BASKETBALL
FOR MEN

About the author

Glenn Wilkes has been head basketball coach at Stetson University since 1957 and has compiled a coaching record that places him among the top twenty collegiate coaches in the nation.

In addition to his basketball coaching success, he has written numerous articles on basketball for coaching journals and has authored two other books, *Winning Basketball Strategy* (1959) and *Basketball Coach's Complete Handbook* (1962). His most recent work is a fifty-minute cassette tape written for the individual player entitled "How to be a Great Basketball Player."

He directs one of the South's oldest basketball schools for young boys and girls each summer and is the founder and director of the highly successful Stetson Basketball Coaching Clinic.

Wilkes earned his undergraduate degree from Mercer University and his M.A. and Ed.D. degrees at George Peabody College.

BASKETBALL FOR MEN

Physical Education Activities Series

Glenn Wilkes
Stetson University

Third Edition

Wm C Brown Company Publishers
Dubuque, Iowa

Consulting Editor

Aileene Lockhart
Texas Woman's University

Evaluation Materials Editor

Jane A. Mott
Smith College

Copyright © 1967, 1972, September 1977 by
Wm. C. Brown Company Publishers

Library of Congress Catalog Card Number: 76-49419

ISBN 0—697—07075—1

Printed in the United States of America

Contents

Preface

Basketball is a thrilling game, exciting for both the participant and the spectator. Because the equipment is inexpensive and the game so popular, opportunities to play or to watch basketball are very numerous.

Information applicable to both the beginner and the more advanced player is given in the following pages. The fundamentals are explained and illustrated. Mastery of these fundamentals is absolutely necessary, for they are basic to any level of play—good body mechanics, good ball handling and excellent footwork are prerequisites to more advanced play. In addition, strategy and team tactics for both the offense and defense are emphasized. The player should always remember that basketball is a *team* game and that the *individual* succeeds only as much as the *team* succeeds.

Self-evaluation questions throughout the book afford the reader typical examples of the kinds of understandings and levels of skill that he should be attempting to acquire. The learner should consider these as examples and should pose additional ones as a self-check on his progress. Since the order in which the content of the text is read and the progression used by the teacher or coach are matters of individual decision, the evaluative materials are not always positioned according to the presentation of given topics. In some instances the reader may find that he cannot respond fully to a question until all the material has been studied or more playing experience has been acquired. He should therefore return to such troublesome questions or physical challenges from time to time until he is sure of the answers or has developed the skills called for, as the case may be.

What basketball is like

1

Basketball is a team sport played by millions the world over, and its popularity seems to increase constantly. It is one of the world's fastest sports and accomplished play requires speed, stamina, and a high degree of skill. It can be enjoyed on an amateur basis, however, in which case intensive training or previous experience is not required.

College teams play the game on a court 94′ × 50′. An 18- inch cylinder called the "basket" or "goal" is attached to a 4′ × 6′ backboard at each end of the court. The objective of each team is to score by causing the ball to go through the basket that is defended by its opponents. A successful shot during regular play is called a field goal and scores two points. An unguarded shot from the free-throw line, awarded for fouls made by the opponents, is called a free-throw or foul shot, and counts one point. There is no other method of scoring.

Since the only way to score is by shooting the ball through the opponent's basket, considerable emphasis is placed on the development of shooting skills. A variety of shots is used and these are discussed in succeeding chapters of this book.

The ball may be advanced from one end of the court to the other either by passing or dribbling. Passing the ball is throwing it from one player to another. Dribbling the ball is bouncing it on the court in a way that will enable the player to advance it. More emphasis is placed on passing than on dribbling because the ball can be advanced quicker by this means; in addition, clever passing enhances teamwork and makes a team more difficult to defend against. Adolph Rupp, the renowned onetime University of Kentucky coach, considers passing the most important fundamental of the game.[1]

A team is comprised of five players. When on offense a team uses a variety of plays or maneuvers that are designed to gain a clear shot at the basket. Once

1. Adolph F. Rupp, Rupp's Championship Basketball, 2d. ed. (Englewood Cliffs, N.J.: Prentice-Hall, Inc., 1957), p. 27.

a shot is taken, the offensive team attempts to have several of its taller players in position to rebound any missed shot.

When a team is on defense, its members may use a variety of defenses to prevent its opponents from getting an open shot at the basket. They may play a man-for-man defense, in which each player goes with his assigned opponent wherever he goes, or they may play a zone defense, in which each member of the team is assigned a particular area of the floor to defend. A combination of man-for-man and zone defenses may be used; in addition, a team may guard its opponents all over the court or fall back near the basket it is defending. No matter what type of defense is used—when the opponent does shoot, the object of the defense is to rebound any missed shot in order to keep the opponent from obtaining possession of the ball and thus getting additional scoring opportunities.

Since both the offensive and defensive teams are fighting for possession of the ball after missed shots, it follows that a primary method of obtaining the ball is by rebounding. Most coaches feel that the team which "controls the boards" will win the majority of the time; considerable attention therefore is placed on rebounding, both offensively and defensively; consequently tall players, and those with excellent jumping ability, are sought as players.

The game is played rapidly and the ball usually changes hands every fifteen or twenty seconds as the result of a score, a rebound, or a violation. Modern basketball shooters have become quite proficient and team shooting percentages are increasing constantly. This has resulted in high scoring games at virtually all levels of play.

The frequency of scoring, the fast moving pace, and rules that are easily understood have combined to make basketball one of the most popular spectator sports. Top college and professional teams regularly play before crowds of 10,000, and some of the larger college arenas seat as many as 18,000 or more. Brigham Young University now has an arena that seats 22,000 and that has, on numerous occasions, been filled to capacity. The University of Kentucky opened its new 23,000 seat Rupp arena in late 1976 and was sold out for every game during the 1976-77 season. It is not uncommon for high school gymnasiums to have provision for several thousand spectators.

What is basketball like? It's fast, exciting, fun to play and enjoyable to watch. In the pages which follow a more detailed description of the game will be given so that you can play the game for fun and watch it with maximum enjoyment.

Skills essential for
every player

2

There are specific skills that must be learned if you are to participate in basketball. How proficient you must be varies with the level of play. All players, however, must be able to perform certain basic shots, pass and receive the ball, dribble, pivot, rebound to a certain extent, and have a fundamental understanding of defensive skills.

Since a basketball team is made up of participants playing several positions, the degree to which each specific skill must be developed varies with each position. A guard will have to excel in ball handling and dribbling more than in rebounding. A forward or center will not be required to handle the ball as much as a guard, but he must shoulder much more of the rebounding responsibilities.

HOLDING THE BASKETBALL

Before the ball can be shot, passed, or dribbled, it is important to know how to hold it. Holding it improperly will result in faulty execution of other fundamentals.

The most important thing to remember is that *the palms of the hands should never touch the ball.* The ball should be held in the fingers with the fingers spread comfortably but as widely as possible (fig. 2.1). The ball is held in this manner whether one is shooting or passing.

Shooting is the most important fundamental in the game of basketball! Without good shooters, a team may possess Cousy-type passers, superb dribblers, excellent rebounders, and other strong assets but may still find it difficult to win consistently. Many coaches feel that shooters are "born" and not "made" and the brilliant touch of some of the nation's great shooters today lends support to this argument. Surely some players do possess the "touch" that other players strive a lifetime to achieve. However, the vast majority of good shooters

Fig. 2.1 Holding the Ball.

are "made" shooters who have combined sound shooting fundamentals with countless hours of practice to develop themselves into good percentage shooters.

Secret to Good Shooting

Is there a secret to good shooting? If such a secret exists, it is this: countless hours of *practice, practice,* and *more practice!* Why do all coaches love to see goals nailed to the sides of garages in students' backyards? Simply because these goals afford opportunities for hours and hours of shooting practice by prospective basketball players. Probably more shooters have been "made" in backyard practice than ever have been made in gymnasiums.

Basic Types of Shots

There are three basic shots that all players should learn:

1. The lay-up shot
2. The jump shot
3. The free-throw or foul shot

The Lay-up Shot　　The basic shot is the lay-up shot which is taken close to the basket at the end of a drive or after receiving a pass from a teammate. Since it is taken from such close range, a high degree of accuracy should be expected.

As you catch the ball, either from a pass or from your dribble, your right foot should be in contact with the floor (assuming you are to shoot right-handed). Carry the ball with both hands to a position outside your right hip and step onto your left foot. As you leap into the air off your left foot, bring the ball to a position above your head and push it to the basket. Your target should be a spot on the backboard twelve to fifteen inches above the goal. The ball should strike this spot and drop softly down through the goal.

If you are a beginner and are just learning to shoot the lay-up shot, it will be best to practice it without using a dribble. Stand on both feet about two steps away from the goal. Step onto your left foot, spring into the air, and take the shot. As you begin to become somewhat proficient at making the shot after one step, move back to a position about even with the free-throw line. Now take three steps without using a dribble. First step onto your left foot, then your right, then your left, and take the shot. As this footwork becomes comfortable to you, add one dribble, using the same footwork.

You must be able to make the lay-up shot while driving to the basket from different angles; therefore, practice the lay-up shot from both the right and left sides of the basket, along either baseline, while driving down the middle, and from other angles as you find you can obtain a lay-up opportunity. Practice the shot with both the right hand and the left hand so that you will be able to shoot with either, depending upon which side of the basket you are driving from.

Avoid developing the habit of "broad-jumping" the lay-up shot. This common error is caused by failure to spring upward as the shot is taken, a move which is needed to brake the forward momentum caused by the drive to the basket. Failure to jump upward decreases the accuracy of the shot because (1) you are not as close to the basket as you could be, and (2) the forward momentum of the body causes the ball to be released harder against the back-board. As you practice the lay-up shot, make certain that the spring from your left foot is upward rather than forward (figs. 2.2, 2.3).

Fig. 2.2 The Lay-up Shot in a Game Situation.

Fig. 2.3 Another Lay-up Shot in a Game Situation. Notice the Shooter's Intense Eyes-on-the-target Concentration.

In addition to "broad-jumping" the lay-up, other common beginners' errors that you must strive to avoid are:

1. *Jumping off the wrong foot.*   If you are shooting with your right hand, it is important to jump or "take off" from the left foot. The opposite is true when shooting with the left hand.
2. *Laying the ball against the board too hard.*   The softer you can lay the ball against the backboard the better your chances of making the shot.
3. *Putting spin or "English" on the ball.*   Any spin on the ball should be that caused by the natural release of the ball and not because of any conscious effort to cause spin.
4. *Shooting the ball too low on the backboard.*   This is one of the more common errors of even accomplished players. They will shoot the ball at a spot no higher than six to eight inches above the goal instead of the more desirable twelve to fifteen inches above.
5. *Holding the ball too loosely on the takeoff.*   Many players hold the ball so loosely on the takeoff that they will miss any shot attempt should any contact from the defense occur. If the ball is held firmly, contact can be made by an opponent and the shot can still be made. This will result in what is commonly called the "three point play"—making the basket and the resulting one free throw awarded for the foul.
6. *Failure to concentrate.*   The shot is so easy that players have a tendency to take the shot for granted, and lose their concentration on the shot. Concentration is important in order to avoid some of the common errors mentioned above.

The Jump Shot   Though the jump shot did not become popular until the early 1950s, it is now considered the most effective shot in basketball.[1] Modern jump shooters have become extremely proficient from as far as twenty-five feet from the basket and, because the shot is taken after the shooter has jumped into the air, it is very difficult to defense. This has resulted in a greater improvement in scoring than any other basketball innovation.

Prior to jumping into the air for the shot, hold the ball in both hands with your shoulders square to the goal and with your knees slightly bent. The jump into the air is made with an upward thrust by both legs. Height of the jump will vary with the individual but, as a general rule, you will not leap as high as possible but will take a smooth, effortless jump into the air for the shot. As the jump is made the ball is brought to a position slightly above and in front of your head. Your left hand should be under the ball for control and the back of your right hand should be facing you. It is very important that your right elbow be under the ball and on a line between you and the basket. Sight at the goal just under the ball. The shot is released by an upward movement of your right elbow and a simultaneous forward push of your forearm and wrist. Your wrist should snap completely forward to provide a good follow-through (figs. 2.4-2.9).

1. Bill Sharman, *Sharman on Basketball Shooting* (Englewood Cliffs, N.J.: Prentice-Hall, Inc., 1965), p. 53.

How many lay-up shots can you make in thirty seconds? Can you make twenty consecutive lay-up shots alternately with the right and left hands and from alternate sides of the goal?

Fig. 2.4 The Jump Shot. Notice the Position of the Right Elbow and the Intense Concentration of the Eyes on the Basket.

Fig. 2.5 The Jump Shot Just Before the Release of the Ball.

Fig. 2.6 The Jump Shot Just After the Release of the Ball. Notice the Follow-through Wrist Action of the Shooting Hand and That the Eyes Are Still Concentrating on the Target.

Balance is very important to the success of the shot. Many shooters fall forward, sideways, or backwards when taking the jump shot; this decreases accuracy and often leads to offensive fouls. You should initiate the shot from a balanced position and jump *straight upwards.* Be sure to practice the jump shot from three situations: (1) from a stationary position, (2) after a dribble, and (3) after cutting to receive a pass. Balance and the upward jump are more difficult in the latter two situations but are of no less importance.

JUMP-SHOOTING HINTS:

1. *Always practice shots you will shoot in a game.* If you play center or forward, it is foolish to spend a great deal of time practicing shots from the guard position, for example.

Can you make five consecutive jump shots from a distance of fifteen feet? twenty feet? Can you do the same off a dribble?

2. Practice shooting *under game conditions* if possible.   If you can find an opponent to challenge, the competition will be beneficial. If you are shooting alone, use your imagination to dream up games that will challenge you to do your best and that will involve earning a score.
3. *Never "force" the shot.*   If you are closely guarded, pass to someone else or make a maneuver to get open for the shot.

Fig. 2.7 The Jump Shot in a Game Situation.

Fig. 2.8 Another View of the Jump Shot in Actual Play. Notice the Shooting Arm Is Fully Extended on the Follow-through.

Fig. 2.9 The Jump Shooter Has Just Released his Left Hand From the Ball and Is Beginning His Shooting Motion.

Competition makes goal-shooting practice more realistic and interesting. Can you devise one or two games suitable for three or four players?

4. *Learn to relax when shooting.* The more practice you get under competitive situations, the easier it will be for you to relax when shooting.
5. Never attempt "wild" or "crazy" shots.
6. Always *follow through.*
7. *Do not shoot when a teammate is in a better position to shoot.*

SHOOTING GAMES:

There are a number of games or contests you can play with a teammate that will add competition and interest to shooting practice. Among these games are:

1. *Twenty-One.* Start at a spot approximately twenty feet from the basket. Shoot a long jump shot, then retrieve the ball and shoot a lay-up. The long shot counts two points, the lay-up shot counts one point. If both shots are made, continue shooting. The first player to reach a total of twenty-one points is the winner. Variety can be added by not allowing a short shot until a long shot is made and by requiring that the player's last shot be a long shot.

2. *Basketball Golf.* Draw nine circles in various locations around the court. Attempt to make a shot from each circle, shooting only one shot from each. Your score is the number of shots made.

3. *Riskit.* This game is similar to Basketball Golf. If you miss a shot, you can have a second chance. However, if you miss the second shot, you must return to the starting point. The first player making a shot at all nine circles is the winner.

4. *Horse.* This is one of the most popular playground games. One player shoots. If he makes the shot, his opponent must duplicate the shot. If his opponent misses, he gets the letter *H.* The object of the game is to make your opponent spell out the five letters of the word *Horse.*

The Free Throw or Foul Shot   Because every participant will be fouled at one time or another, it is necessary for all players to be able to shoot free throws or foul shots. There are two major styles of free throws: (1) the underhand, and (2) the push shot which may be taken by either a one-hand push or a two-hand push.

The underhand method has proven to be slightly more accurate and accomplished players may utilize it a great deal. Bunny Leavitt set the world free-throw record using this method when he scored 499 consecutive free throws. Nevertheless, the popularity of this method has greatly declined in recent years and most players now use the push-shot method. This is so because

Which of the two styles of free throw has been found to be more accurate? Do you know why most players elect not to use this style?

the same basic shot which is used in regular play can also be used from the free-throw line, and the additional practice that would be required to develop the underhand method is, as a result, not necessary. However, Golden State's Rick Barry uses the underhand method and has compiled one of the outstanding free-throw shooting percentages in the National Basketball Association. Attention being brought to this method by Barry, and his games on nationwide television, may result in more players using this method.

THE PUSH-SHOT METHOD.   If the shot is a one-hand push shot, you stand with your right foot approximately one inch behind the free-throw line with your left foot approximately twelve inches back. The feet should be shoulder width apart and the knees slightly bent. Balance must be maintained, though most of the weight will be forward. The ball is held by both hands and just in front of the face. As when shooting the jump shot, your left hand should be under the ball in order to control it and the back of your right hand should be facing you. Elbows should be in close to your body. The shot is initiated by a simultaneous straightening of your knees and raising of your right elbow. As the elbow is raised, a forward push of your forearm and snap of your wrist pushes the ball toward the basket. The ball should leave from the index and forefinger of your right hand and complete follow-through should leave your arm fully extended and your wrist broken completely over so that your palm will be facing downward.

THE UNDERHAND METHOD.   Stand with your feet spread shoulder width apart and with the toes of each foot about one inch behind the free-throw line. Your knees should be slightly bent and the ball should be held in a position between your legs with arms fully extended downward (fig. 2.10). Thumbs point away from your body. The first move of the shot is to bend your knees to an almost 45-degree angle. The legs are then straightened and the ball is shot toward the basket with an upward swing of your arms as in figure 2.11. After the ball is released your fingers should point at the basket with your thumbs upward.

FREE-THROW SHOOTING HINTS:
1. It is extremely important for you to learn to *concentrate* when shooting the free throw.
2. When you go to the free-throw line for a shot, take two or three deep breaths before shooting. This will help you to *relax*, an essential to good free-throw shooting.
3. All players can learn to shoot free throws well if they are willing to *practice* enough.
4. Practice under *competitive* situations whenever possible. Challenge teammates to free-throw shooting contests often. If shooting alone, try to make

Fig. 2.10 Starting Position for Underhand Free Throw.

Fig. 2.11   The Underhand Free Throw Just After Release of the Ball.

Fig. 2.12 Ordinary Free-throw Stance for a Right-handed Shooter.

as many consecutive free throws as possible or a certain percentage of the number attempted. Competitive practice aids concentration and will result in improved shooting in an actual game.

Shooting Essentials

Varying techniques are used when shooting each type of shot. However, several essentials for all types of shots are listed below:

1. *Good Vision.* A player must be able to see the goal clearly if he is to develop the consistent depth perception that will enable him to shoot a good percentage. Players who wear glasses all day and then remove them for the basketball game that night cannot expect to be good shooters. Contact lens or glass guards may be bothersome but may prove necessary to assure good shooting ability.

2. *Good Hand Position.*   The ball should be held with fingers spread widely and with the *palms off the ball.*
3. *Concentration.*   When the shooter takes aim for the basket, he must be concentrating on the shot with his eyes centered on the target.
4. *Relaxation.*   Muscles must be functioning properly during the shooting motion. Tenseness will prevent this.
5. *Follow-through.*   The shooter must follow through on all types of shots. This is a common error committed by many shooters and *its correction often improves shooting percentage tremendously.*
6. *Confidence.*   *The shooter must believe that he is going to make the shot.* Ask the great shooters and they will tell you that they never take a shot that they don't *think* they're going to make! If the shooter is putting the ball in the air and "hoping" it will go in the basket, he and the team would be far better off if he passed to someone else for the shot attempt.

PASSING AND RECEIVING THE BALL

Passing and receiving the basketball are skills as important as shooting. By clever passes the ball can be advanced into the area of the court where high percentage shots can be obtained, but the most clever pass can be completely ineffectual if the receiver cannot catch the ball and a fumble results.

If the ball is to be properly received, the hands should be cupped so that the heels of the hands will be three or four inches apart, fingers spread comfortably and thumbs almost parallel. The arms should be extended. As the ball strikes the hands, you should "give" with the pass—in other words, flex the elbows in such a manner that your hands move in toward your body as the ball is received. This is tremendously important, for stiff arms and hands result in many fumbled passes. To emphasize this point, think of throwing a basketball against a brick wall. What will it do? Rebound back to the passer, of course! Now think of throwing a basketball against a blanket hung over a clothesline What will happen to the basketball? The blanket will "give" and the ball will drop to the ground, not rebounding to the passer. This is the type of softness pass receivers must have for proper ball handling.

To be a good pass receiver you must learn to "look the ball into your hands." In other words, you must keep your eyes on the pass until it strikes your hands. Failure to do so is a major cause of fumbled passes. Players actually start to dribble or pass before the ball gets to them.

Another cause of poor receiving is a lack of concentration. Players often take the pass for granted, assuming it can easily be caught. The assumption would be correct if you did not have to contend with interference from the defense.

Receiving is a fundamental skill just as important as passing. One is dependent on the other. You must place a great deal of emphasis on learning to make good passes but you must place just as much emphasis on learning to receive the ball properly.

Fig. 2.13   A Player in Passing Position.

Types of Passes

Three types of passes are essential for all players:

1. Chest pass
2. Bounce pass
3. Flip pass

Chest Pass   The most common pass in basketball is the chest pass. In fact, when we think of passing as a part of basketball we immediately think of this type of pass. The ball is held in both hands with the fingers comfortably spread. *Remember, the palms of the hands do not touch the ball.* Your thumbs point at an angle to each other. The ball is directly in front of your chest. The pass is made with a forward thrust of your arms and a simultaneous snap of your wrists. Complete arm extension is necessary for proper follow-through. The palms of your hands should be downward at the completion of the pass. It is important that the pass be thrown so the receiver can receive it above his waist but not above his head.

Bounce Pass   The bounce pass is made in the same manner as the chest pass; however, it is pushed down to the floor and bounces up to the pass receiver. This is a good pass to use in order to pass by a taller opponent or to feed a teammate who is in close to the basket. Considerable practice is necessary to enable you to know how far from the receiver the ball should strike the floor. If it strikes the floor too far away from the receiver, the ball will float into the air and be easily intercepted. On the other hand, if the ball strikes the floor too close to the receiver, it will be difficult for him to handle the pass (fig. 2.14).

Flip Pass   The flip pass is necessary during a close exchange of the ball, as, for example, on a close weave when the ball is "flipped" softly from one player to another. The pass is made by placing the passing hand directly under the

Tape a small square approximately two feet in diameter on a smooth wall. Tape a larger square around it three feet in diameter. Stand fifteen feet way and make chest or bounce passes at the target. Count two points for the ball striking the center square and one point for the outer square.

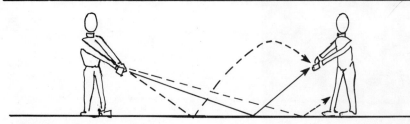

Fig. 2.14 Solid Line Indicates the Correct Path of the Bounce Pass While the Broken Lines Indicate Incorrect Paths. The Bounce Pass That Strikes the Floor Too Close to the Receiver Usually Bounces Too Low for Easy Handling, While the Bounce Pass That Strikes the Floor Too Far Away from the Receiver Bounces Too High into the Air and Is Easily Intercepted.

ball and flipping the wrist so that the ball will flip into the air. The ball should be flipped softly *upward*, not outward, and should not be flipped more than a few inches above your hand. This type of pass is easily received by a player cutting to the basket. It is used by pivotmen in feeding cutters and the dribbling screener uses it to pass to players cutting by the screen.

PASSING HINTS:
1. Don't "telegraph" the pass. Look one way and pass another.
2. Fake the chest pass and throw the bounce pass. Fake the bounce pass and throw the chest pass.
3. Follow through.
4. Keep the palms off the ball.
5. Throw the flip pass in close quarters.
6. Pass to the receiver on the side away from his defensive player.
7. Pass to the region of the receiver's chest. Passes are more easily handled there and the receiver is in position to make another pass without adjusting to the height of the ball.

DRIBBLING

The dribble is used to advance the ball downcourt, to initiate play patterns, to make drives to the basket, and to move into good shooting position when pass receivers are closely guarded.

The dribble technique is relatively simple and can easily be mastered with proper practice. The dribble is executed by pushing the ball to the floor with a snap of your wrist and downward motion of your forearm. Fingers should be

Dribble chairs. Place five or six chairs in a straight line approximately five feet apart. Dribble in and out of the chairs using the right hand when dribbling on the right side of the chair and the left hand when dribbling on the left side of a chair. Keep the head and eyes straight ahead and **do not look down at the ball.**

comfortably spread in order to achieve maximum control of the dribble. It is important that you learn to dribble (a) *without looking at the ball,* and (b) *with either hand.* Dribbling without looking at the ball enables you to see teammates who might break into the clear. The ability to dribble with either hand is necessary so you can drive in any direction, therefore making the defensive players' task more difficult.

It is also necessary to learn both (1) the speed dribble, and (2) the control dribble. The speed dribble is used when you must advance the ball quickly downcourt and no defensive players are harassing you. Your body should be in an upright position and the ball is pushed out in front of you. When defensive players are near and the ball must be protected, use the control dribble. In this case your knees should be bent so that your body will be low and the ball is dribbled lower and closer to the body (fig. 2.15).

Fig. 2.15   Dribbling Position. Knees Bent. Head up. Eyes ahead.

It is almost as important for you to learn *when* to dribble as *how* to dribble. The dribble is often misused, and it is detrimental to the morale of the team when a player monopolizes the ball by over-dribbling. Though no ironclad rule can be made indicating when to dribble, a general guide is to *avoid dribbling when it is more advantageous to pass.* Remember that the ball can be moved much more quickly by passing than by dribbling, and that quick movement of the ball makes a team very difficult to guard.

DRIBBLING HINTS:
1.   If a pass is more advantageous to your team, do not dribble.
2.   Do not look at the ball when dribbling.

Dribble tag. With two, three, or more friends, each with a ball, play "tag." Whoever is "it" must attempt, while dribbling, to tag someone. The other players must attempt to keep away from "it" while also dribbling. Boundaries are established, using the out-of-bounds lines on half-court. Anyone going outside the boundary must become "it." Play games using both the right hand and then the left hand.

3. Learn to dribble equally well with either hand.
4. Do not develop the habit of taking a dribble immediately upon receiving a pass. Save your dribble as a threat to your opponent.
5. Do not "bat" the ball. Push it to the floor.
6. Never attempt to dribble between two defensive players.
7. Remember—it is as important to know *when* to dribble as *how* to dribble.

PIVOTING

Proper pivoting techniques must be mastered by all players in order to prevent "traveling" or "walking" violations. The rules of the game allow the player holding the ball to step in any direction with one foot while keeping the other foot, called the *pivot* foot, at its point of contact with the floor. The player may continue to move the other foot as long as the ball of his pivot foot remains in position. The primary purpose of the pivot is to enable the ball handler to pivot his body between an opponent and the basket to protect the ball. Once the pivot foot has been established, it cannot be changed without involving an intervening dribble or pass.

The *simple pivot* is normally used at the end of a dribble, and is the only pivoting technique the beginning player needs to master. The dribble is received into both hands with one foot in advance of the other. Your rear foot becomes the pivot. You can move your front foot in any direction as long as the ball of your rear foot remains in contact with the floor (fig. 2.16). It is very important that the pivot be made on the ball of your foot; a pivot on your heel results in a violation.

REBOUNDING

Rebounding missed shot attempts is one of the most important facets of the game. The team that controls the majority of the rebounds usually emerges victor despite weaknesses in other areas of play. It is because good rebounding is so necessary that the tall player has become so important to the game. Though the position a player plays will determine how often he is in position to rebound, all players must learn proper rebounding techniques. Throughout the game all players will have an opportunity to rebound either offensively or defensively, and usually both.

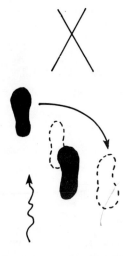

Fig. 2.16   The Simple Pivot. Dark Area Represents Position of Offensive Player's Feet at the End of His Dribble, While the Dotted Lines Indicate His Foot Position After He Has Pivoted Away From Defensive Player X to Protect the Ball.

Defensive Rebounding   When an opponent shoots, the defensive player must immediately prepare for the defensive rebound. He cannot wait until it is determined whether the shot is missed. He must immediately position his body between his opponent and the basket to prevent an offensive rebound and the resultant second shot attempt. This maneuver—keeping the body between the opponent and the basket—is referred to as "blocking" or "screening" off the boards, or a "block out."

As the shot is taken, step into the path of your opponent, pivot your body so that your back is against him, and use a slide step to keep between him and the basket. Your eyes must be on the ball; therefore you must "feel" your opponent with your rear and back. Your elbows should be out, your hands up, and your knees flexed, ready to spring. As the ball starts coming downward, jump into the air as high as possible, keeping your body spread in order to take up as much room as possible. Grab the ball tightly with both hands and light on the floor onto the balls of your feet. You must keep the ball moving to keep your opponent from obtaining joint possession of it and getting a "jump ball." Be careful not to sling your elbows back and fourth in your efforts to protect the ball. Though this affords good ball protection, the method became so popular several seasons ago that there was considerable danger of bodily injury. Because of this, the rules were amended making it a violation to sling the elbows in this manner. You can keep the ball moving without slinging your elbows and this ball movement is very important for protecting possession.

Offensive Rebounding   The offensive player must go for the rebound the instant a shot is taken. In fact, the great offensive rebounders *anticipate* a shot attempt and *move into rebounding position before the shot is taken.* When this can be done, it is rather difficult for the defense to use blocking tactics to prevent the offensive rebound.

An objective of the defensive rebounder is to "block" or "screen" his offensive opponent off the boards; the offensive player therefore must use his

Fig. 2.17   Offensive Rebounding in a Game Situation.

abilities in an effort to counteract this defensive objective. Since the defensive player must *feel* the offensive player in order to have continuous success at blocking off, the offensive player must prevent this by moving away from the defensive player, even if it means that he must step away from the basket. Once no contact exists between the offense and defense, the offense can move toward the basket with less interference. Faking in one direction and cutting in another is very difficult for the defense to handle. Clever fakes and changes of direction are essential ingredients of the successful offensive rebounder.

INDIVIDUAL DEFENSE

As in all team sports, a strong team defense is required for successful play. Though a variety of team defenses may be used, strength will depend a great deal on the specific defensive skills of the individual members of the team. This individual defensive ability depends upon four major factors: (1) Stance; (2) Footwork; (3) Position; and (4) Vision.

Stance   Individual defensive play demands quick movement to counteract offensive maneuvers. This quick movement is almost impossible unless the defensive player maintains the correct defensive stance. Assume a position with one foot in advance of the other and with your knees bent so that your rear will be low. Your back should be straight and your head up to permit good vision. One hand is usually held up ready to block an opponent's shot attempt while the other hand is lower and in position to harass any attempted pass (fig. 2.18). From this stance, you can best utilize the footwork that will enable you to move quickly to another position that may be required by quick movement of your opponent.

Footwork   Proper defensive footwork centers around the *slide* step. When this step is used, your legs are never crossed and you remain in a position which makes possible quick changes of direction. Assuming you are sliding right with

What part of the opponent's body should you watch to avoid being misled by a fake?

Fig. 2.18   Individual Defensive Stance.

your opponent, your first movement would be with your right foot, sliding it approximately twelve inches to your right. Your next move would be to slide your left foot into a position very close to your right. Your right foot would then be moved again and so on. The reverse would be true for the slide left.

Defensive footwork is similar to that employed by the boxer. To approach an opponent, you simply slide forward, keeping one foot in advance of the other. To defend a drive or cut, use the slide to retreat backwards toward the basket. Remember, to be able to slide properly, your weight must be kept low, balance must be maintained and your legs should never be crossed.

Position   No matter how correct a defensive player's stance or how quick his footwork it can all be to no avail if he fails to maintain the proper floor position. Generally, this requires the defensive player to *remain between his opponent and the basket at all times*. If the defensive player does this, he can prevent his opponent from cutting or driving in a straight line for the basket and he can remain in position to harass any attempted shot.

The actual floor position of the individual defensive player will vary with the position of the ball. If you are guarding an opponent who has the ball you will remain on a line between the opponent and the basket. If you are guarding an opponent who does not have the ball you will also maintain this position, but you should move slightly toward the ball. Figure 2.19 pictures this technique. Dotted lines represent a straight line between the offensive player and his goal. O1 has the ball and is being guarded by X1. Notice that X1 is directly on the dotted line. Player O2 without the ball is being guarded by X2, who

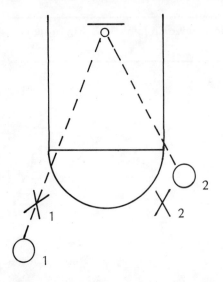

Fig. 2.19   Proper Defensive Position.

moves slightly off this line and toward the ball in order to be in a better position to block any cut to the basket by O2 and to prevent a pass to O2 in the areas close to the basket. If a pass were made from O1 to O2, X2 would move on to the line between his opponent and the basket and X1 would slide toward the ball.

Vision   Proper vision is as important to defensive play as it is to offensive play. It enables the defensive player to see both his opponent and the ball at the same time. In addition, it enables him to perceive offensive screens and defensive situations that may require his help.

Peripheral vision is important. Players with good eyesight should be able to see action within an arc of almost 180 degrees. If the defensive player is guarding an opponent with the ball, he should focus his eyes on the offensive player's belt or midsection. This is very important because the midsection is the only part of his body the offensive player cannot use in faking. By use of peripheral vision, the defensive player should be able to see action both to his left and right.

If the defensive player is guarding an opponent who does not have the ball, he should focus his eyes on a spot approximately midway between his opponent and the ball (fig. 2.20). By doing this, his peripheral vision will allow him to see both his opponent and the ball, an important requirement for man-for-man defensive play.

DEFENSIVE HINTS:

1. Keep the knees bent, the rear low, and the back almost straight. The head should remain erect.
2. Stay off your heels.
3. Do not cross your legs when moving across court.
4. Watch the opponent's belt or midsection. It cannot be used to fake.

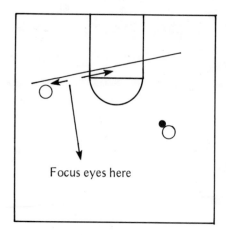

Focus eyes here

Fig. 2.20 When Guarding an Opponent Who Does Not Have the Ball, the Defensive Player Should Focus His Eyes on a Point Between the Ball and His Respective Opponent. This Enables Him to Be Able to See Both His Opponent and the Ball at the Same Time and to See Other Action Within an Arc of Almost 180 Degrees.

5. Never leave the floor until after the opponent has gone into the air for the shot.
6. Never turn your head to look for the ball. If you do, your opponent may cut by you to the basket.
7. Prevent your opponent from receiving the ball near the basket.
8. Talk on defense. Don't be a silent sister.
9. When your opponents get the ball, *think* defense immediately.
10. Study your opponent. Learn his strengths and weaknesses and play accordingly.

Fig. 2.21 A Defensive Player Attempting to Block a Jump Shot in a Game Situation.

Fig. 2.22 Defensing the Jumpshooter in Actual Play.

Better players master these techniques

3

Mastery of the techniques described in chapter 2 will enable the average individual to enjoy participating in basketball; however, more advanced players master other techniques that enable them to achieve even greater success. Though not absolutely necessary for the average player, a knowledge of and at least minimum skill in these other techniques will increase anyone's enjoyment of the game.

SHOOTING

The lay-up shot, jump shot, and free throw have become necessary for all players. Another shot used extensively by advanced players is the *hook* shot.

The Hook Shot   The hook shot is taken from close range and is begun *with the back to the basket.* For a right-hand shot, step onto your left foot and extend your right arm *fully away from your body* with your right hand under the ball in order to achieve control. Keep your left hand on the ball as long as possible (fig. 3.1). As you step and turn toward the basket, bring your right arm straight upward in a swinging motion to the basket. Release the ball at the height of the extended arm. Backspin is imparted to the ball as your wrist snaps in a complete follow-through. Most hook shooters shoot the ball against the backboard and let it carom into the goal. The target on the backboard is approximately the same area as for the lay-up shot, some twelve to fifteen inches above the goal.

The hook shot is difficult to master for the average player; however, since the shot is taken with the arm fully extended away from the body, it is so difficult to guard that work on it—particularly by taller players who play near the basket—can pay big dividends in scoring ability. The range of the hook shot is limited and it should not be attempted when more than ten to twelve feet away from the basket.

Mark a 12-inch circle on the wall and stand 40 feet away. How many times can you hit the target in ten attempts using the baseball pass? using the hook pass?

Fig. 3.1   The Hook Shot.

PASSING

One-Hand Push Pass   Advanced players usually become proficient at passing with one hand. One of the most popular types of one-hand passes is the *one-hand push pass* in which the player—usually a good ball handler—uses one hand to simply push the ball to a teammate. It can be either an air pass or a bounce pass and has a definite advantage over the two-hand pass because it can be more easily made from the side of the body. This pass is also very effective off a dribble since it can be passed without the dribbling hand coming in contact with the ball.

Baseball Pass   The baseball pass is used to pass to teammates cutting downcourt and is essential to the repertoire of members of fast-breaking teams. The pass is made with one hand, similar to the regular baseball throw. To begin the pass bring the ball with the right hand to a position behind your right ear and your weight on your right foot. As you pass downcourt, your weight will shift forward onto your left foot. You should be careful to avoid imparting side spin on the basketball since this makes it curve and decreases accuracy.

Hook Pass   The hook pass is made in the same manner as the hook shot. To hook pass right-handed, step onto your left foot, extend your right arm fully away from your body with your right hand under the ball, and pass the ball in a sweeping motion directly over your head. A wrist snap is important to assure proper follow-through.

The pass is difficult to control; however, it is excellent for passing the ball over an opponent and out to a teammate after a defensive rebound. Like the baseball pass, the hook pass is used quite extensively by the fast-breaking team. The ability to make this pass with either hand adds to your effectiveness.

Two-Hand Overhead Pass   The two-hand overhead pass is very effective for passing the ball over the head of a defensive player and into a teammate in the pivot area. The ball is held in both hands with arms almost fully extended over the head. The heel of each hand faces toward the target. Make the pass by thrusting both arms forward and snapping both wrists in order to impart speed to the pass. At the completion of the pass, your fingers should face the target (fig. 3.2, 3.3).

DRIBBLING

While all players should learn to dribble with either hand, better players must develop proficiency in three other dribbling techniques:

1. The Switch Dribble
2. The Reverse or Spin Dribble
3. The Change-of-Pace Dribble

All three techniques are used for changing direction quickly. The switch dribble is faster but does not allow as much protection of the ball as does the reverse dribble.

Fig. 3.2   The Two-hand Overhead pass.

Fig. 3.3   The Two-hand Overhead Pass in Actual Play.

The Switch Dribble   The switch dribble simply involves changing the hand with which you are dribbling in order to change direction or to afford better ball protection. The switch is made in front of your body and must be made as low as possible to prevent the defensive player from deflecting the dribble. As you dribble with your right hand, push the ball sideways in front of your body so that it bounces into position on the left side of your body where it can be taken with your left hand. Your left hand continues the dribble. This skill is essential for a quick change of direction, but since it is done in front of your body, considerable practice is required to be able to protect the ball from the defensive player (figs. 3.4, 3.5, 3.6, 3.7).

Fig. 3.4   Beginning the Switch Dribble.

Fig. 3.5   The Switch Dribble (cont.). Ball Has Been Bounced to Floor by Right Hand and Is About ot Be Received by the Left Hand.

Fig. 3.6   The Switch Dribble (cont.). Ball Has Now Been Received into Left Hand and Dribble Is Continued.

Fig. 3.7 Protecting the Dribble in a Game Situation.

The Reverse Dribble   The reverse or "spin" dribble also makes possible a change of direction; however, throughout the reverse dribble your body is kept between the ball and the defensive player and therefore more protection is given the ball than is possible with the switch dribble. Since the reverse dribble requires your body to turn 180 degrees in order to execute the change of direction, it is slower than the switch dribble. It usually is used when a defensive player is guarding the dribbler tightly and overplaying in the direction the player is dribbling.

If you are dribbling to your right you must plant your weight on your left foot and swing your right foot in an 180 degree turn while the dribble is being changed to your left hand. After the complete turn of the body you will be

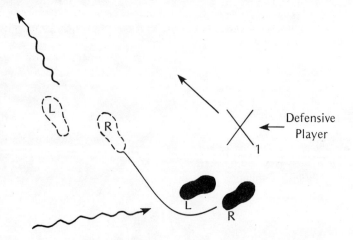

Fig. 3.8 Footwork for the Reverse or "Spin" Dribble.

advancing toward the left and dribbling with your left hand. The accomplished player can often swing his right leg in such a manner as to "trap" the defensive player and thus provide a clear drive to the basket.

The Change-of-Pace Dribble   The change-of-pace dribble technique is simply varying the speed you are moving while dribbling. By varying your speed you keep the defensive player guessing and prevent him from making moves to steal the ball. The change-of-pace is a very good scoring weapon. As you dribble toward the basket at full or near full speed, slow down coming to almost a complete stop. When the defensive player stops also, you then go at full speed toward the basket. This "stop-and-go" dribble maneuver often results in letting you drive by your defensive player for an easy lay-up shot.

DRIBBLE DRILLS:

1. *The switch dribble drill.*   Place a chair at the free-throw line. Using your right hand, dribble to the chair. Then switch dribble to your left hand, and drive in for a lay-up shot. Return to the starting position and repeat the drill, this time using your left hand first.

2. *The reverse dribble "square" drill.*   Start in a corner of the court. Dribble along the sideline to a point even with the free-throw line. Reverse dribble and dribble to the free-throw line. Reverse dribble and dribble along the lane line to the baseline, then reverse dribble and return to the starting point. Repeat this several times using the right hand, then dribble in the opposite direction using the left hand.

3. *The "imagination" dribble drill.*   Dribble up and downcourt using a variety of dribble moves. Imagine that the defensive player is guarding you. Use the change of pace to get by him, then use the speed dribble to drive downcourt for a lay-up. On the return trip, use the control dribble to the sideline and when your imaginary opponent overplays you, reverse dribble by him. Use your imagination to enable you to employ all of the dribble moves into a full court game that will not only improve your dribble skills but will also be great for your physical conditioning.

THE ONE-ON-ONE OFFENSIVE SITUATION

No matter how well you may be able to execute the basic shooting and passing fundamentals, if you do not develop the necessary offensive maneuvers to free yourself from your defensive opponent, you will find it rather difficult to score. The ability to play "one-on-one," as these maneuvers are commonly called, will make it necessary that you develop quick starts and stops, fakes and clever changes of direction, and the ability to shoot quickly and from various angles on the court. The ability does not come easily but requires considerable practice before any degree of success can be achieved against even the average defensive player. Advanced players spend a great deal of time playing "one-on-

Using your preferred hand can you dribble the length of the court without looking at the ball? Can you do the same with the nonpreferred hand? When alternating hands?

one" with each other, and most basketball team offenses provide opportunities for the better players to get their defensive opponents into "one-on-one" situations.

You should develop the following abilities in order to be a good one-on-one offensive player:

1. *Fake right, shoot.* Fake a drive to your right with a short "jab" step of no more than twelve inches. As the defensive player steps back, go up for the jump shot. It is important that the "jab" step be short, since a long step will leave you with your feet too wide apart and not in jump-shooting position.

2. *Fake left, shoot.* After a short "jab" step straight ahead with the right foot, fake your head left as if to drive left. As the defensive player retreats, go up for the jump shot.

3. *Fake right, drive left.* After a short jab step right, immediately drive left without faking the shot.

4. *Fake left, drive right.* Instead of faking right, fake a drive left using your head. As the defensive player moves to your left, drive right.

5. *Fake right, fake left, drive right.* Make a short jab step right, then fake a drive left with your head. As the defensive player moves to your left, drive to the right.

6. *Fake left, fake right, drive left.* Fake a move to the left with your head. Then make a short jab step right. As the defensive player moves to your right, drive to the left using the crossover step described in figure 3.8 and illustrated in figure 3.9.

7. *Fake right, fake shot, drive right.* Make a short jab step right, raise the head and upper body and look at the basket as if your were going to shoot. As the defensive player comes forward, drive by him to the right.

8. *Fake right, fake shot, drive left.* Make a short jab step right, raise the head and upper body and look at the basket as if you were going to shoot. As the defensive player comes forward, drive by him to the left using a crossover step.

The Long First Step   On all of the one-on-one moves described above, an important key to their success is a long first step. After you have made your fake, your first step to the basket must be as long as possible in order to drive you by the defensive player. This is very important, so practice this long step until it becomes automatic.

The Crossover Step   In order to be able to fake one direction and drive another, you must learn the *crossover step* (figs. 3.8, 3.9). This step is necessary

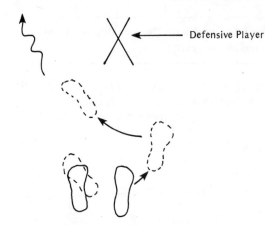

Defensive Player

Fig. 3.9 The Crossover Step. With the Pivot Foot to the Left, the Offensive Player Fakes a Drive to the Right by Either Stepping to the Right or Faking His Head and Shoulders Right. He Quickly Pivots on His Left Foot and Simultaneously Crosses His Right Foot Over So That His Initial Step on the Drive Left Will Be with His Right Foot.

in order to avoid walking or traveling violations. If the pivot foot is the left foot and you fake right and drive left, your first step left must be made with the right foot; hence the necessity of the crossover step.

NOTE: All of the one-on-one moves described above are executed before you dribble or at the beginning of your dribble. Therefore, it is important that you not put the ball immediately on the floor after receiving a pass. If you have "used up your dribble" no amount of faking will enable you to drive by your opponent.

Head-faking Since the above moves are used at the beginning of a dribble, you must also develop moves to be used at the end of your dribble. Suppose you fake left and drive right toward the basket. Your opponent—diagnosing your moves—moves into proper defensive position. It will then be necessary for you to use additional one-on-one type moves to get your shot off. These moves at the end of a dribble center around "head faking." Fake the shot by

Fig. 3.10 The One-on-one Drive in Actual Play. Player No. 24 Has Used the Crossover Step to Drive by the Defensive Player. Notice That He Is Dribbling with the Hand Away From the Defensive Player to Better Protect the Ball.

Have you practiced faking with the head and with the jab step until you can easily do the combinations suggested in the text?

looking at the basket and faking the head once or twice. The head fake will enable you to get the shot off even though you may be closely guarded. In addition, you will often draw fouls since the defensive player may leap into the air and fall on you.

Progress can be speeded up

4

In any sport, the mastery of fundamentals is absolutely essential to the development of skill. Basketball is no exception. Fundamentals must be mastered for any degree of playing success. The University of Kentucky's great former coach, Adolph Rupp, says that if there is a secret in successful basketball that secret is drilling on fundamentals.[1] The ability to execute these fundamentals is not learned overnight. Many long hours of work are required; however, progress can be speeded up if a player has a sincere desire to learn basketball skills. Basic is the desire to learn; with that desire, even the less coordinated player can achieve considerable skill—without that desire to learn even the most athletically inclined will attain little success.

Seek Professional Help and Advice

The player anxious to learn basketball can speed up his progress if he is sure of what he should practice, knows drills which are recommended for the development of these skills, has a basic understanding of the game, and knows when the different skills should be used. These things can best be learned by talking with professional people who are closely associated with the game and by reading the wealth of literature available in books and in athletic coaching journals. Local coaches and physical education instructors will be glad to suggest methods of practicing skills and usually will be able to answer any questions you may have. Accomplished players can also give many helpful hints on how they developed their abilities.

Practice With a Purpose

Through talks with coaches and players and by reading literature on the game, decide on a definite procedure for developing fundamental skills. Work diligent-

1. Adolph F. Rupp, *Rupp's Championship Basketball* (Englewood Cliffs, N.J.: Prentice-Hall, Inc., 1948), p. 23.

Which trajectory, A or B, is more appropriate when closely guarded? Which trajectory is more accurate? Which requires more strength?

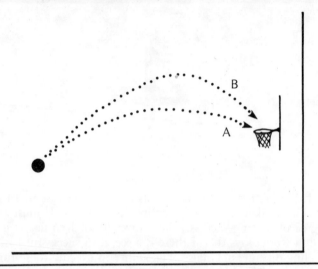

ly on each of these, and as proficiency is acquired in one, increase the amount of time placed on weak areas. *Practice daily.* If the gymnasium is not always available, there are now outdoor hard-surfaced courts in most communities which afford adequate practice areas. It would be wise to purchase a rubber basketball for use on these outdoor courts. If no court is available, it is rather economical to purchase a goal and backboard and erect these at your home.

The big key in developing skills is *dilligent practice.* This requires work; there is no substitute for work in any sport, especially if advanced skill is desired.

Take Advantage of Every Opportunity to Play

Skills are of no use unless they can be used in actual competitive situations. The ability to pass the ball accurately is no good if you cannot pass it by a defensive player. The ability to shoot accurately is of no use if you do not develop the ability to free yourself from your opposing guard. One other player is all that is necessary for a competitive situation. Play as much "one-on-one" as possible. The more "one-on-one" play you can obtain, the quicker you will develop your overall basketball skills.

"One-on-one" play is, however, not enough. Team play is necessary for success. "Three-on-three" is excellent for developing both individual and team basketball skills.

Do not neglect "five-on-five" play. If possible, register for play in intramural leagues or participate on junior varsity teams. If these are not available, investigate the possibility of playing in local city recreation leagues, YMCA leagues, and church leagues. Diligent practice is essential, but playing on actual teams is equally important.

Watch Games and Films

An excellent method of learning is to watch games in which accomplished participants are playing. If a college or professional team is nearby, seize every opportunity to see them play. Watch individual players and study their techniques. Study team strategies and patterns in order to achieve a clearer understanding of the game. If no college or professional team is nearby, watch local high school teams—they too will present good opportunities for learning.

Films provide another excellent avenue for learning the game. All of the college and professional teams and many high school teams have film available that they are usually willing to lend for the publicity value. Do not hesitate to write to coaches of the various teams for help in securing these game films.

Keep in Good Physical Condition

Since you will run about three miles during an average basketball game, you must have a great deal of strength and endurance, especially in your legs. Following are some recommended exercises that will help you achieve optimum physical condition:

1. *Cross-country running.* Develop the ability to run for several miles up and down hills and over all sorts of terrain. Start out with a short distance and gradually increase the distance until you can run at least three miles without stopping.
2. *Wind sprints.* While cross-country running is great for your endurance, the running of wind sprints not only aids endurance but helps you increase your speed as well. Run short dashes (50-yard) as hard as you can, then walk a similar distance, before running another dash at full speed. Continue for several sprints.
3. *Rope jumping.* Rope jumping is very good for endurance and leg strength and also helps develop your coordination and footwork.
4. *Fingertip push-ups.* Do push-ups off the fingertips. This will strengthen your fingers and the muscles used in shooting and passing. In addition, it will reduce finger injuries, a common basketball injury.
5. *Bench jump.* Stand beside a bench approximately sixteen to eighteen inches high. Jump over it and without stopping return to the starting position. Continue jumping over the bench without stopping—twenty to twenty-five times. Rest briefly. Then repeat. This exercise will add leg strength and increase your jumping ability.
6. *Stops and starts.* Sprint forward, stop, sprint forward. Continue.
7. *Backward running.* Run backwards. This will not only help in your conditioning but will improve your body balance.
8. *"Boxer's slide" or "shuffle" step.* This is the basic footwork necessary for good defensive play. Slide forward, backwards, left, and right, as quick-

ly as possible without crossing the feet and while keeping the body low. Start with slides for one minute and increase until you can slide step for several minutes.

9. *Squeeze a ball.* A tennis ball or rubber ball is all you need. Squeeze it for five to ten minutes daily to increase finger and lower arm strength.

10. *Weight training.* Strength and body bulk is important to a basketball player, particularly to those who play near the basket. An organized program of weight training can help your overall physical condition and add the strength and necessary weight. Your coach or physical education instructor can recommend certain weight-training exercises for you. Those exercises most often used by basketball players are:
    a. Toe raises
    b. Half squats
    c. Military press
    d. Bench press
    e. Arm curls

Get a Proper Warm-Up Before Practice

Your body can be in peak condition yet can be susceptible to injury. To help prevent injuries, make certain to engage in a proper warm-up before every practice period. Jogs around the court and stretching types of exercises prior to any practice that requires quick starts, stops, and jumping are excellent activities. Remember, it is rather difficult to achieve speedy progress if your body is hampered by a pulled muscle or a similar injury.

Take Care of Your Feet

It has often been said that a basketball player is no better than his feet. How true! The sudden starts and stops required by the game often result in blisters and foot injuries to those who do not take proper care of their feet. To help prevent these type injuries it is very important that you wear shoes and socks that fit properly, and that they be kept as clean as possible.

Offensive patterns of play

5

Basketball is a team game that requires a great deal of cooperation among players for successful execution of team offensive patterns. In efforts to develop offenses difficult to defend against, intelligent coaches have developed a host of team offenses. The more common are discussed in this chapter.

KEY TO DIAGRAMS

Defensive player	X	Pass	--------->
Offensive player	◯	Dribble	~~~~~~>
Path of player	——————>	Screen	————⊣

MAJOR ESSENTIALS FOR A SOUND TEAM OFFENSE

The major essentials necessary for a sound team offense are:

1. Movement of the ball
2. Movement of the players
3. Obtaining the good shot
4. Obtaining the second shot
5. Maintaining floor balance
6. The one-on-one situation

Movement of the Ball   All offenses must move the ball if the defense is to be penetrated. This is true whether the defense is man-for-man, zone, or a combination of both. The team that passes the ball slowly from one player to another is simply playing into the hands of the defense, providing an opportunity for the defense to shift, sag, fight through or around screens, or make some other move to counteract an offensive screen or maneuver. On the other hand, the team that keeps the ball moving from player to player will make the defense keep constantly on the move to compensate. It is far easier to attack the defense when it is kept moving than when it is allowed to stand virtually motionless and concentrated around the basket.

Movement of Players   One of the qualities that often distinguishes great players from good ones is the ability to be dangerous when not in possession of the ball. Most players can make an offensive move if they possess the basketball. Far fewer players remain dangerous after giving up ball possession.

The sound offensive pattern will allow for movement of players in conjunction with movement of the ball. Constant movement, fakes, and cuts are necessary. When players remain in one position and pose no offensive threat, most defenses quickly take advantage and use sinking or double-teaming tactics to congest a more dangerous area. This is far more difficult when all offensive players are kept on the move and each constantly poses a threat to the defense.

Obtaining the Good Shot   The sound offense must work for the good percentage shot. Few teams win consistently if they continually violate this principle. The team that is overly anxious to shoot, and has poor play patterns, which result in sub-par team play, will find its members taking the bad shot often—and will find themselves on the short end of the score at game's end.

The sound offensive pattern will be designed so that its primary objective is to get the good shot. What is meant exactly by "good" shot? When can a player shoot with the complete knowledge that the shot is a good one? First, the player must have the ability to shoot the shot. What may be a good shot for one player may be a bad shot for another. The twenty-foot jump shot by a guard could be a percentage shot whereas the same shot taken by a big center could very well be a bad shot. Second, rebounders must be in position for the shot to be considered a good shot. Few things are more irritating in basketball than the player "gunning the ball up" from twenty feet out with no one even near the rebounding area.

Obtaining the Second Shot   Many coaches maintain that this is the chief essential of offensive play. Statistics show that the team that consistently gets the offensive rebound and the resulting second shot attempt usually is successful. Therefore, the offensive pattern must be planned so that at least three players are in position to rebound a shot attempt. Three rebounders in position, provided these players are grounded soundly in offensive rebounding fundamentals, will usually result in an adequate number of second-shot attempts. Obviously, the play patterns should be so designed as to get the better rebounders into the rebounding area.

Maintaining Floor Balance   All good offensive patterns will eliminate congestion insofar as possible. To do this, the floor must be kept balanced. The type of offense being played will determine just where players must be to keep the floor balanced. In general, when two or three players are standing close together (unless part of a play pattern as on a single or double screen), they are easily defensed. One player can defense two standing close together and allow one defensive player to sag and congest the scoring area. Proper floor spacing or balance will help prevent this.

Proper floor balance not only includes offensive balance but defensive balance as well. Provision must be made in every play pattern for players to remain out to prevent fast break opportunities by the opponents. Of course, the number of players needed for defensive balance responsibilities will depend on the particular opponent. A fast-breaking opponent will require two players back for maintenance of defensive balance whereas the slow-breaking or ball-control opponent will require only one player back for proper defensive balance.

The One-on-One Situation   The sound offense will include opportunities for the one-on-one situation in order to take advantage of the scoring abilities of the better offensive players and to capitalize on weak defensive players. The offensive guard who fakes a drive and shoots the jumper, the forward who drives the baseline for a lay-up, and the center who rolls for a score are all executing one-on-one scoring maneuvers. The stereotyped offense that does not allow such individual scoring moves is greatly reducing its effectiveness and can more easily be scouted and defensed.

Offensive Patterns

The Single Pivot Offense   Fig. 5.1 depicts the single pivot offense, probably the most common offensive pattern known to basketball. A and B are the guards, C the center, and D and E are the forwards. The guards are usually smaller than the forwards and centers, but are usually better ball handlers and quicker and better outside shooters. The forwards and centers as a rule are taller players and do more shooting around the basket and handle a great part of the rebounding responsibilities.

Three simple plays from the single pivot formation are shown in figures 5.2, 5.3, and 5.4. Of course, they can be run from either side of the court and either

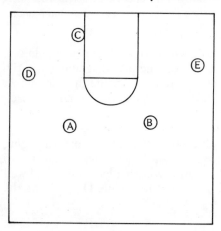

Fig. 5.1   Basic Single Pivot Offensive Formation.

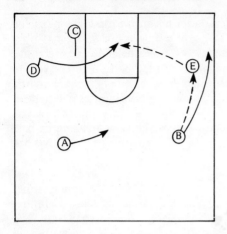

Fig. 5.2 Single Pivot Play. Player B Passes to E Who Passes to D Cutting Off Screen Set by C.

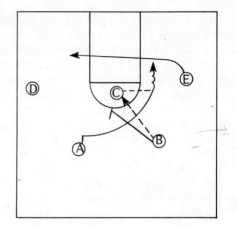

Fig. 5.3 A Single Pivot Play Using the High Post. E Clears to the Left Side as B Passes to C. B Cuts Off C and A Cuts Using B as a Screen. A Receives Pass and Drives for a Lay-up or Jump Shot. This Play Is Referred to as a "Split the Post" Play.

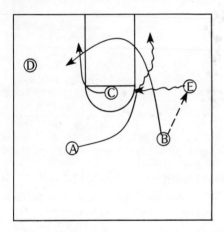

Fig. 5.4 The "Kentucky Second Guard" Play From the Single Pivot. B Passes to E and Clears Through. E Drives to Free-throw Line and Gives a Flip Pass to A who Drives for a Lay-up or Jump Shot.

guard can initiate the offense. The play shown in figure 5.2 is a simple one involving a center screen for the offside forward. The play diagrammed in figure 5.3 is what is commonly called a "split the post" play while the play shown in figure 5.4 is the "second guard play" that was popularized by famed coach Adolph Rupp while at the University of Kentucky.

The Double Pivot Offense   The double pivot offense is shown in figure 5.5. This offense is used when a team has two tall players they would like to keep close to the basket and three smaller players who can handle the ball well and shoot from the outside. A, B, and C are the guards while D and E are the pivot players.

Figures 5.6, 5.7, and 5.8 show three simple plays from the double pivot formation. Figure 5.6 is a "split the post" play while figure 5.7 is a double screen for a guard. Figure 5.8 shows a double screen for one of the post players.

The Tandem Post Offense A third type of offensive pattern popular with basketball teams throughout the country is illustrated in figure 5.9 and is re-

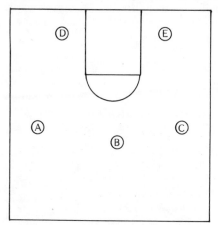

Fig. 5.5 Basic Double Pivot Offensive Formation.

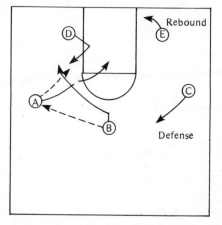

Fig. 5.6 Double Pivot Play. Player A Pases to D and Sets Screen for B Cutting Outside.

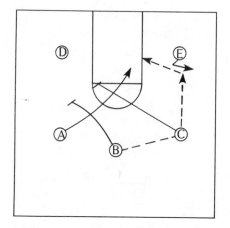

Fig. 5.7 B Passes to C Who Passes to E. B and C Set a Double Screen for A Cutting to the Basket. If A Is Not Open, B Can Cut Back Toward the Ball for a Possible Pass.

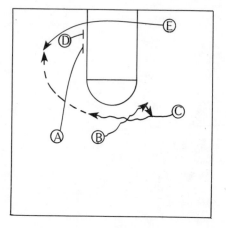

Fig. 5.8 A Double Screen for One of the Pivot Players. B Makes a Dribble Hand-off to C. A and D Set a Double Screen for E Who Receives a Pass from C.

ferred to as the tandem post or 1-3-1 offense. A is referred to as the "point man," B and C are the "wing men," while D is the "high post man," and E the "low post man." The tandem post is a particularly good offense to use when a team has an outstanding guard to direct the offensive attack and two good post men who can operate well close to the basket.

Figures 5.10, 5.11, and 5.12 show simple plays from this formation. Figure 5.10 illustrates a simple screen on the ball with a double screen option while figure 5.11 shows a double screen for the low post player. A rear screen play is shown in figure 5.12.

The Shuffle Offense   A pattern type offense that has become rather popular during the last few years is the shuffle offense developed by Bruce Drake while he was head coach at the University of Oklahoma, and more recently popularized by Auburn University in the Southeastern Conference. The offense is unique since players must learn to play all positions. Because of this fact, the

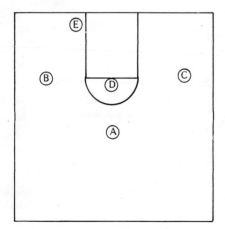

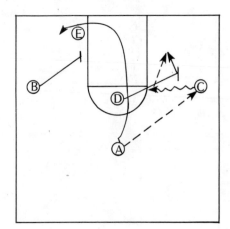

Fig. 5.9   Basic Tandem Post or 1-3-1 Offense.

Fig. 5.10   A Passes to C and Cuts Off D Looking for Possible Pass to C. After A Cuts By, D Moves Out to Set a Screen for C. As C Dribbles Off Screen, B and E Are Setting a Double Screen for A. C May Shoot or Drive to the Basket, Pass to D on a Roll Play, or Pass to A Behind the Double Screen.

Fig. 5.11   A Passes to C and Cuts Outside to Take a Return Pass. C and D Move Across the Lane to Set a Double Screen for E.

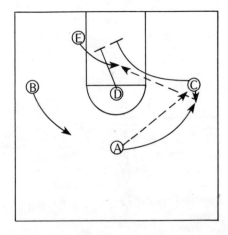

If all team members are similar in height, which type of offense might be particularly good to try? Does this offense require more or less player versatility than the single pivot offensive formation?

shuffle offense is a particularly good offense for a team not possessing the good tall player but which has balanced height.

Figure 5.13 shows the initial formation of the shuffle attack. Note that the player in each position has a specific number. Number 3 passes to 2 who passes to 1. Number 3 cuts off the screen set by the post man 5. This is referred to as the first option. As 3 cuts into the pivot area, 4 makes a V cut on the baseline and cuts high toward the ball into a more or less second option position. After passing to 1, 2 sets a screen for 5 who cuts to the top of the circle for a possible pass from 1. This is the third option. If no shot is obtained as a result of this play, the players are now in the position shown in figure 5.14, and are ready to run the offense from the right side of the floor. The reader can quickly see that one of the distinct advantages of this offense is the fact that the players do not have to return to their original starting positions to continue the offense.

The Weave   One of the most common patterns of play is the weave offense that has been so popular in the eastern sector of the United States. The weave can be used from any of the basic formations presented earlier in this chapter. It is a continuity type pattern that requires good ball handling, clever passing

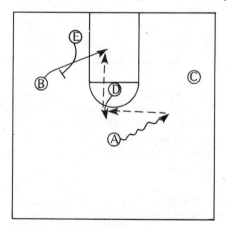

Fig. 5.12 A Dribbles Toward C and Makes a Quick Pass to D Stepping to the Top of the Circle. As the Pass Is Made, E Moves Up to Set a Rear Screen for B Who Cuts for the Basket. If B Is Not Open, D May Pass to E Who Should Have a Good One-on-one Opportunity.

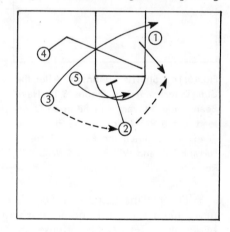

Fig. 5.13 Basic Shuffle Offense. Pattern Begins with Overload to Side, in This Case the Left. Number 3 Passes to 2 Who Passes to 1. Number 3 Cuts Off 5's Screen. Number 4 Then Cuts as Shown Toward the Ball. Number 5 Moves to Top of Circle Off 2's Screen.

and quick cuts to the basket. Figure 5.15 shows the basic weave pattern from the single pivot formation.

The Passing Game   The passing game has been a basketball offense for a number of years but only recently has it begun to stir up interest throughout the nation. Henry Iba of Oklahoma State was among the first to use the offense successfully and Don Haskins used it in winning the 1965 NCAA championship at Texas Western (now Texas-El Paso). North Carolina's Dean Smith was one of the first coaches in the Eastern part of the country to use it with any success, and it is Smith who has probably done more to stimulate interest in the offense than any other coach. Bobby Knight used it to coach the 1976 Indiana Hoosiers to the NCAA championship and more and more teams undoubtedly will be using the offense in the near future.

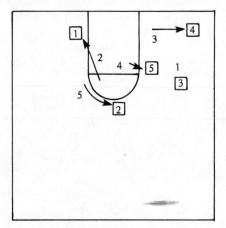

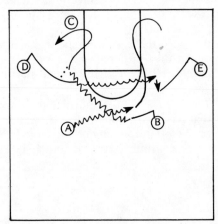

Fig. 5.14   Shuffle Continuity. After the Cuts Diagrammed in Figure 5.13 Have Been Made, Players Will Be in an Overload to the Right Side of the Floor and Ready to Continue the Pattern. Here, 3 Has the Ball and Will Pass to 2 Who Will Relay to 1.

Fig. 5.15   The Weave. Player A Dribbles and Passes Off to B. After Making the Pass A Cuts Down Middle for a Possible Return Pass. Player B Looks for A, Then Dribbles Over and Hands Off to D Who Continues Over to E. Weave May Be Three-, Four-, or Five-man Weave.

The passing game is a free-lance type offense. Players have freedom to move about the court and are not required to cut to certain areas as required by set play offenses. The offense emphasizes movement of the ball, movement of players, shot selection, and team play. At the same time, it minimizes dribbling and one-on-one individual play. It can be run from any formation.

Though players are given a certain amount of freedom, all passing game offenses operate within a strict set of *rules*. It is very important that players know these rules and abide by them, for if players violate them, the offense will turn into a helter-skelter undisciplined free-lance attack. Some of the rules common to most passing game offenses are:

1. *You must move every time a pass is made.* This may sound simple but it is a rule that is violated often. Players have a tendency to stand still after passing.
2. *Move with a purpose.* When a player moves, he must move with a purpose, not aimlessly. He moves to screen for a teammate, to cut to the basket looking to get open, to fake a screen and then cut to the basket, always with a purpose.
3. *No more than two dribbles after the offense is initiated.* This helps to build up team play and eliminates excessive dribbling and the resulting individual play.
4. *At least four passes must be made before a shot is taken unless the ball goes to the low post area.* Four passes help to instill team play and the feeling that if a player gives up the ball he will get it back.
5. *Anytime a player is overplayed by the defense, he must cut to the goal or screen for a teammate.* This rule is important to keep players from "fighting pressure."
6. *Always make the easy pass.* This may sound simple, but it may be the most important rule. What is an easy pass for one player may be a hard pass for another. As players learn to make the "easy" pass, their turnover rate decreases greatly.
7. *After a player receives a pass, he must face the goal, and hold the ball at least two seconds before he passes.* Players have a tendency to receive the ball and pass too quickly. The two-second pause gives things a chance to develop inside and gives the passer time to see them.
8. *If a player cuts into the post area, he must move out if he does not receive the ball within two seconds.*

There are several keys to the success of the passing game offense. They are the following:

1. *Movement of the ball.* It is very important that the ball be kept moving. Each player should hold the ball for two seconds to give things a chance to develop, then he should move it. The more the ball is moved, the more difficult it is for the defense.
2. *Player movement.* We are referring to moving without the ball. It is a basic fundamental skill that players need to learn. Without proper player movement the defense can prevent good ball movement. Both ball movement and player movement are dependent on one another.
3. *Shot selection.* It is absolutely necessary that players take good shots. Excellent ball and player movement will make no difference if a team's shot selection is poor.
4. *Team play.* Since movement of the ball and movement of the players are so important to the passing game's success, team play becomes even more important. Bad shots and individual play will result in poor ball movement and poor player movement.

The Fast Break

A very popular pattern of play throughout the country is the fast-break offense. It is a tactic sometimes referred to as "getting there firstest with the mostest." The fast break is a planned attempt by the offense to get the ball into its scoring area so quickly that its members will outnumber the opposition. The fast-break team hopes to rebound a missed shot by the opponent and pass it quickly downcourt as the players break at full speed into their scoring area.

The most common fast-break situations are the three-on-two and the two-on-one. Occasionally the defense will get caught without anyone back and the offense will get a one-on-none situation. Other outnumbering situations are four-on-three and five-on-four.

Figure 5.16 shows a typical three-on-two fast-break pattern. Player A rebounds the ball and tosses it out to player B. Player B passes to the middle to player C and cuts down the right sideline. While this has been taking place, player D has cut hard down the left sideline to fill a lane and the players outnumber the opponents three to two.

The two-on-one situation is illustrated in figure 5.17. Player A rebounds the ball and tosses it out to player B. As B advances the ball downcourt he sees that the defense has only one player back. B can either advance the ball downcourt on the dribble or pass it to player C who advances it downcourt (as indicated). As C reaches an area approximately even with the free-throw line, he passes the ball to B for the lay-up. Of course, what C does with the ball will

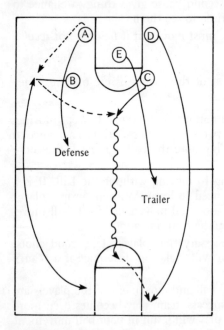

Fig. 5.16   Typical Three-on-two Fast-break Pattern.

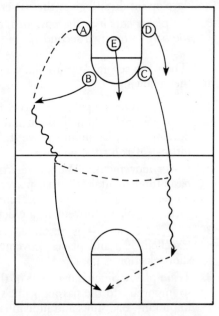

Fig. 5.17   A Two-on-one Fast-break Pattern.

On a fast-break attempt, what should B do with the ball?

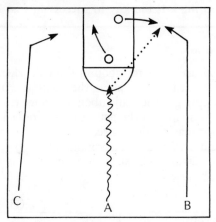

be determined by how the lone defensive man plays. If the defender plays toward B, C may fake the pass and drive for the lay-up himself. Considerable drill practice in both the three-on-two and two-on-one is necessary for players to be able to react properly.

The key to the successful fast break is in the speed with which the outlet pass is made after a rebound. If the rebounder holds the ball for a few seconds, he enables the defensive team to fall back into proper position. On the other hand, if the rebounder quickly passes it out to his teammates good opportunities are presented for them to get the ball down floor before the opponents have gained defensive position.

The fast break is colorful to watch and is enjoyed greatly by the spectators. It is largely responsible for the popularity that professional basketball enjoys today. It is true that handling the basketball at full speed does lead to ball-handling errors. Many coaches, particularly those in junior and senior high schools, feel that the advantages gained by the fast break do not offset the errors made in attempting it; therefore, these coaches do not allow their players to use the fast break as an offensive weapon. However, players love the fast-breaking game and as they become more and more skilled, it is being used more and more.

When to Fast Break

Fast-breaking opportunities may be found after the following situations:

1. A missed field goal or free throw by the opponents.
2. A successful field goal or free throw by the opponents.
3. A bad pass, double dribble, or other loss of ball possession by the opponents.
4. A jump-ball situation.

Can you describe four situations that may afford opportunity for a fast break? What do you think is the key to success in fast breaking?

Out-of-Bounds Situations

A team must have special plays to inbound the ball when they have it out-of-bounds either under their basket or along the sideline. The first purpose of the special play is to simply get the ball inbounds; however, as the ball is taken out-of-bounds there is a lapse in the action that affords a good opportunity to call a special play that may result in a score.

Figures 5.18 and 5.19 show two commonly used plays from under the basket while figures 5.20 and 5.21 show plays used along the sideline.

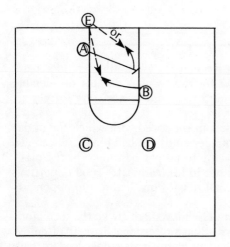 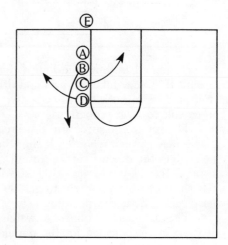

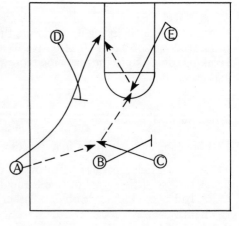

Fig. 5.18 A Sets Screen for B Who Cuts Toward Ball. If Defense Does Not Switch, Pass Is Made to B. If Defense Switches, Pass Is Made to A Rolling Back Toward Ball.

Fig. 5.19 Vertical Formation. D Cuts Toward Corner After D Cuts, C Cuts into Lane. B Then Moves Out to Receive Pass if D or C Are Not Open.

Fig. 5.20 B Screens for C Who Receives Inbounds Pass. C Passes to E Who Passes to A Cutting Off Rear Screen Set by D.

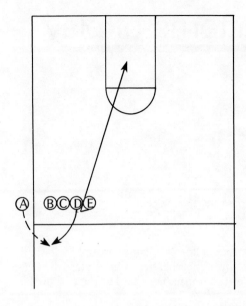

Fig. 5.21 Four-in-a-line Horizontal Formation. Excellent for Late in the Game When Leading and the Opponent Has to Have the Ball. If E is Closely Guarded, He Cuts to the Basket for Possible Pass and Lay-up. If E is Not Closely Guarded, He Simply Breaks into the Backcourt to Receive Inbounds Pass.

Defensive patterns of play

6

The importance of sound team defensive play in championship basketball cannot be overemphasized. The major difference between the average basketball team and those who ride the crest of the tournament trail at the end of the season lies in ability to play defense!

There are basically two different types of defenses: the man-for-man defense, and the zone defense. The man-for-man defense assigns a player a specific opponent to guard and he is to guard this opponent wherever he may go in the opponent's offensive pattern. In the zone defense, the defensive player is assigned an area or zone on the court to guard rather than a particular opponent. He then guards any player who comes into his zone or area.

Though the man-for-man and zone are *basically* the two defenses in basketball, they have been combined; different shifts and maneuvers have been employed with each. The result is quite a number of different defenses which are used in the game.

TEAM DEFENSIVE ESSENTIALS

Regardless of the type of defense a team may use, certain essentials must be adhered to for the defense to be successful:

1. *Team members must have a desire to play defense.* Because of the nature of the game and the tremendous amount of publicity and public favor given to the high scorers, most players prefer to play offense. However, defense can be the great equalizer. When the offense is having a bad night—and this will invariably happen—good sound defense can produce victory. But good sound defense cannot be played unless team members *want to play defense.*
2. *Correct defensive stance and footwork must be used by all team members.* No player can play good defense in an incorrect stance or with faulty foot-

work. Since a good team defense is dependent on not one or two players but on five working as a coordinated unit, improper stance or footwork by any one of the five can reduce greatly the effectiveness of the team defense.

3. *Correct positioning must be maintained by all team members.* A player cannot expect to defense an opponent unless he maintains proper floor position. In man-for-man defenses, this will mean that he usually will be between his respective opponent and the basket. If his opponent breaks into the area near the basket, it will be necessary for him to play between his opponent and the ball to prevent him from receiving the ball in such a dangerous scoring position. If the team defense is a zone, each player must be in the proper floor position in his zone and must make the proper shifts with the movement of the ball. An incorrect shift will result in improper floor position and a weakness in the team defense. One player out of position can nullify the work of four other players and weaken an otherwise sound defensive unit.

4. *Team members must talk to one another to be able to combat the variety of situations that may occur.* Talk is a valuable asset to a good team defense. The player who will not yell out to teammates to warn them of special situations will impair the effectiveness of the team defense, despite the fact that he himself may be a good individual defensive player. Calls, such as "watch the screen," "screen left," "switch," "stay," "rebound," and "slide through" are a few of the many needed to insure correct defensive action for the variety of offensive screens and maneuvers that may be faced.

5. *Definite responsibilities and techniques must be established for meeting the various types of offensive maneuvers that may be encountered.* A good team defense will be prepared to meet all types of offensive formations whether it be a single pivot, double pivot, or other offensive formation. Definite techniques and responsibilities must be established for meeting the various play patterns that go toward making up these team offenses. Definite methods are necessary for handling the various types of screens, the "split-the-post" situation, the "give-and-go," the "screen-and-roll," the "double screen," and other offensive plays. These methods must be developed on the practice floor and cannot be left to chance during the game.

6. *Definite rebounding assignments must be made.* Rebounding assignments begin with a shot by the opponent. If the defense is a man-for-man, each defensive player must screen (box out) his opponent so that he will be between this opponent and the basket. Failure to do this by any one member of the defense can result in an easy basket for the opponent. If the defense is a zone, players must be certain of rebounding areas and must attempt block-outs of opponents in their respective areas.

MAN-FOR-MAN DEFENSE

Use of the man-for-man defense permits the making of defensive assignments on the basis of height, position, speed, and offensive ability. The team's best

B has the ball. The defense is sagging to prevent a pass to E. What should B do with the ball? What is a good way to get the ball to E?

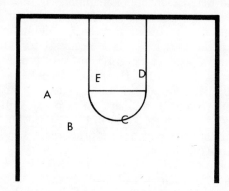

defensive guard may be assigned to the opponent's best scoring guard. The poorest defender may be assigned the opponent's weakest scorer. A slow defensive player may be assigned a slow opponent. Thus match-ups are facilitated and definite responsibility can be charged for scoring by opponents. Individual pride in defensive ability is thereby more easily fostered since each player has a particular opponent to guard and can judge his performance in terms of points scored by this opponent.

General Principles for Man-for-Man Team Defense

Most teams that use the man-for-man defense will use general team defensive principles similar to the following:

1. *Maintain a position between your opponent and the basket unless he is in the pivot area close to the basket.*
2. *Always point or "pressure" the ball.*   One defensive player must be closely guarding the man with the ball at any time he is within shooting distance.
3. *Protect the baseline.*   Most man-for-man defenses concentrate on preventing opponents from driving along the baseline to the basket. For a number of years this was a cardinal rule of all man-for-man defenses. However, in recent years a few teams have built good team defenses without emphasizing baseline protection. For the average team it is, nevertheless, an excellent rule to follow.
4. *Prevent the close shot.*   Good man-for-man defensive clubs seldom give up the open lay-up shot. When a driver gets by his opponent and moves for the basket, he is no longer the responsibility of one man but becomes

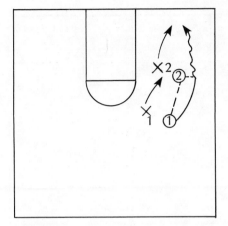

Fig. 6.1 A Common Switching Maneuver by a Man-for-Man Defense. O1 Passes the Ball to O2, Receives a Return Pass, and Drives to the Baseline. X2 Simply Yells "Switch" to His Teammate and Picks Up O1 Driving to the Baseline. X1 guards O2.

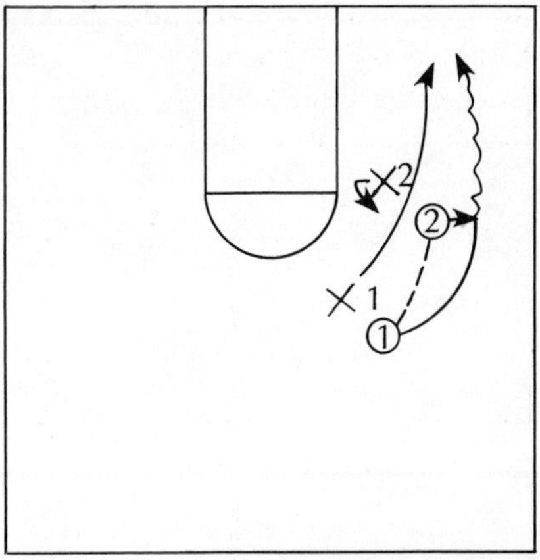

Fig. 6.2 The Same Offensive Maneuver with the Defense Not Switching. As O1 Cuts Outside, X2 Simply Takes a Step Back and Lets X1 Slide Through and Keep His Man.

the responsibility of *all* defensive players. Defensive players must then converge on the basket in efforts to prevent the close shot.

5. *Prevent the second shot.* The game can be won or lost on the backboards. It is mandatory for every defensive player to screen his man off the board in order to minimize the number of rebounds and resulting second shots the offense may obtain.

6. *Screens must be handled with consistency.* This means that a team must practice prior to game play the method it will use in combating screens. If switching is to be used against screens, then switching techniques must be practiced. Figure 6.1 illustrates a common switching maneuver. If players are not to switch, then they must practice fighting through screens and receiving help from their teammates as shown in figure 6.2.

7. *Keep the ball out of the pivot area.* Once a player receives a pass in the pivot area close to the basket, it is virtually impossible to defense him. Therefore, it is imperative that such passes be prevented.

Defensive Positioning

Figure 6.3 illustrates normal man-for-man defensive positions with the ball at the guard position. Notice that **X1** is "pointing" the ball. **X1** and **X4** are "sagging" to help prevent a drive by **O2** while **X5** is preventing a pass to his man in the pivot area. **X3** is "sagging" more than any other player since his opponent is not in position to receive a pass.

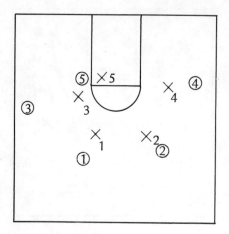

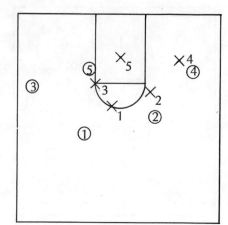

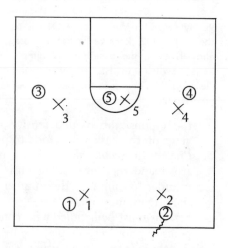

Fig. 6.3   Normal Man-for-man Defensive Positioning with the Ball at the Guard Position.

Fig. 6.4   Normal Man-for-man Defensive Positioning with the Ball at the Forward Position.

Fig. 6.5   The Half-court Man-for-man Press. Defensive Players Stay Very Close to Their Assigned Opponents and When the Dribbler Picks Up His Dribble, All Defensive Players Try to Prevent Passes to the Players They Are Guarding.

The ball is shown at the forward position in figure 6.4. X4 is "pointing" the ball while X5 has moved toward the ball still intent on preventing a pass into the pivot. X1, X2, and X3 are "sagging" to help prevent drives and cuts. Notice that X3 is "sagging" more here than when the ball is at guard position. This is simply due to the fact his man is even further away from the ball.

The position on the court in which defensive players can pick up their opponents can vary. Figures 6.3 and 6.4 show the normal man-for-man defense. However, defensive players can pick up their assigned opponents about three feet outside the defensive circle. The position of pick-up can be moved out to the midcourt line, in which case the defense is referred to as the *half-court man-for-man press* (fig. 6.5). Going farther, the position of pick-up can be made at three-quarter or at full court and the defense referred to as the *three-quarter court man-for-man press*, or the *full-court man-for-man press* (figs. 6.6, 6.7).

Pressing defenses are used in an effort to force the opponent to make mistakes. Such defenses are particularly useful against the weak ball-handling

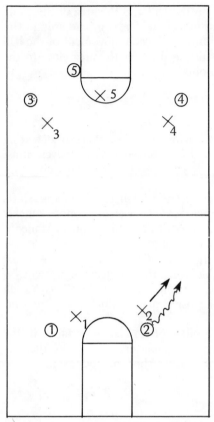

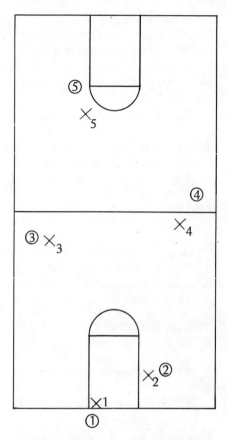

Fig. 6.6   The Three-quarter Court Man-
for-man Press. Defensive Players Attempt
to Prevent Passes to the Players They Are
Guarding.

Fig. 6.7   The Full-court Man-for-man
Press. Defensive Players Pick Up Their
Opponents While the Ball Is Still Out-of-
bounds.

team, the inexperienced team, the poorly conditioned team, and especially against the methodical pattern type team. It is an absolute must when the defensive team is trailing late in the game.

Rather than pressing, the man-for-man defense might sag and jam the defensive basket area. This is referred to as a *sagging* man-for-man defense or *collapsing* man-for-man defense. This type of man-for-man defense is used quite often when an opposing team is weak in outside shooting, or has a high-scoring center.

ZONE DEFENSE

Zone defenses differ from man-for-man defenses in that players are assigned a particular area of the court to defend rather than having to defense a specific opponent. Foremost attention is focused on the ball and the area of the court to be defended. All defensive players mass in assigned areas in and around the free-throw lane and shift as a coordinated unit with each movement of the ball by the offense. This team massing and shifting protects the area close to the basket and makes short shots difficult to obtain.

General Principles for Zone Defense

1. *Players must get into position quickly.* Most offensive plans for defeating the zone include the fast-break. Therefore, zone defensive players must hustle downcourt and into proper defensive position immediately upon giving up the ball.
2. *Players must maintain good individual defensive stance.* The rapid shifts necessary with offensive ball movement can be executed more quickly when proper defensive stance is maintained. In addition, correct stance is necessary to prevent offensive dribble penetration.
3. *Players should keep hands up in position to deflect passes.*
4. *Talk is of utmost importance to be able to handle offensive movement.*
5. *Players must focus their attention on the ball and shift rapidly with each movement of the ball.* No zone defensive player should ever turn his back to the ball.
6. *Prevent the second shot.* This principle is of no less importance in the zone defense than in the man-for-man. Zone players must know their rebounding responsibilities regardless of where a shot may be taken.

Types of Zone Defenses

Four major zone defenses are used by modern basketball teams:

1. 2-1-2 zone
2. 2-3 zone
3. 1-3-1 zone
4. 1-2-2 zone

These zone defenses are pictured in figures 6.8 through 6.13. Zone defenses require that the players move in their area according to the position of the ball. This movement is referred to as *shifting*. Note in figures 6.9 and 6.10 how the 2-1-2 zone has shifted as the ball is passed around the perimeter of the defense. This shifting is necessary in all types of zone defenses.

Pressing Zone Defenses

The normal zone defense picks up the opponent just outside the top of the circle. However, as in the man-for-man defense, the position of pick-up can vary from midcourt to three-quarter to full court.

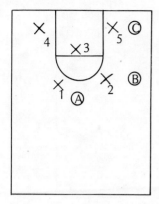

Fig. 6.8   The 2-1-2 Zone Defense.

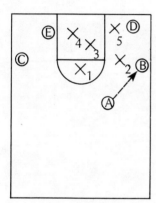

Fig. 6.9   The Shift of the 2-1-2 Zone
with the Ball at Forward Position.

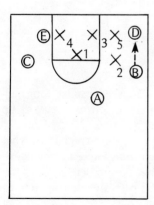

Fig. 6.10   The Shift of the 2-1-2 Zone
with the Ball in the Corner.

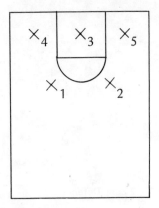

Fig. 6.11   The 2-3 Zone.

Fig. 6.12   The 1-3-1 Zone.

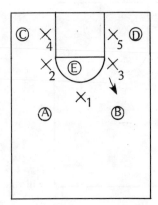

Fig. 6.13   The 1-2-2 Zone.

The most common pressing zone defenses are:

a. The 1-3-1 half court zone press (fig. 6.14)
b. The 1-2-1-1 full court zone press (fig. 6.15)

As with man-for-man presses, these zone presses are used against poor ball-handling teams, the methodical pattern type team in an effort to speed up play, and when the defensive team is trailing late in the game.

The basic move of the zone press sends two players onto the ball in what is termed a *trap*. This leaves an offensive player open somewhere on the court. Therefore a good pass by the offense can result in having the defense outnumbered similar to a fast-break situation. Once this good pass is made it is tremendously important that the defense chase the ball at full speed. This chase of the ball is referred to by coaches as *pursuit*. Many feel that good *pursuit* of the ball is the real key to a successful zone press.

Can you score from position B if your defensive player is dropping back toward the offensive center C?

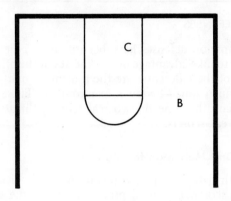

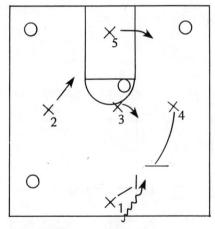

Fig. 6.14   The 1-3-1 Half-court Zone Press. As the Dribbler Crosses Midcourt, X1 and X4 Put on the Trap. X3 cuts Any Pass to the Middle, X5 Protects on the Ball Side of the Lane While X2 Prevents a Pass to the Left Corner.

Fig. 6.15   The 1-2-1-1 Full-court Zone Press. On the Throw-in X1 and X3 Trap the Ball While X4 Prevents a Pass to the Midcourt Area and X2 Protects the Middle of the Court.

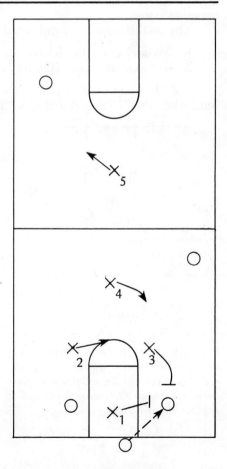

Two combination man-to-man and zone defenses are the box and one and the diamond and one. When would you use each one and how do they work?

COMBINATION DEFENSES

A variety of combination defenses have been used by coaches to combat particular strengths or to take advantage of weaknesses in the offense of opponents. The most popular of these defenses are the four man zone—one man man-for-man and the three-man zone—two man man-for-man. These defenses are effective when the offense has one or two real scoring threats, with their other teammates being weak scorers.

Four-Man Zone—One Man Man-for-Man

In this defense, four defenders play zone and one defensive player is assigned the opposing high scorer. It is used primarily against the so-called "one-man teams" that occasionally are met and is an excellent method for defensing the opposing star.

Two methods are commonly used in playing this defense:

1. Box and One (fig. 6.16).
2. Diamond and One (fig. 6.17).

The "Box and One" is stronger at the guard position and weaker at forward while the "Diamond and One" is stronger at the forward position and

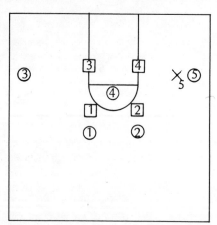

Fig. 6.16 "Box and One" Combination Defense. Defensive Players 1, 2, 3, and 4 Set Up a Four-man Zone Defense While Defensive Player X5 Guards the Opposing Star Player Man-for-man.

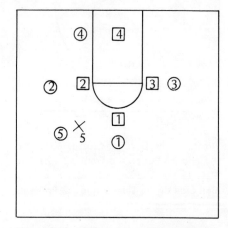

Fig. 6.17 "Diamond and One" Combination Defense. Defensive Players 1, 2, 3, and 4 Set Up a Four-man Diamond Zone Defense While Defensive Player X5 Guards the Opposing Star Player Man-for-man.

weaker at the guards and in the corners. The position played by the opposing star that will be defensed man-for-man will determine which of the two defenses should be played. If the opposing star is a guard, strength will not be needed at the guard position since the one man playing man-for-man will be defensing the star at that position. Consequently, the "Diamond and One" should be selected. However, if the opposing star is a forward, more strength will be needed in the guard defensive area, therefore the "Box and One" is more likely to prove successful.

Three-Man Zone—Two Man Man-for-Man

This defense is an excellent one for the team that has two top threats, so often encountered in amateur basketball. Three defenders play in triangular zone positions and two defensive players are assigned to the two top scoring opponents. Figure 6.18 diagrams this defense. The zone shifts are similar to those made by rear line defenders of the 2-1-2 zone defense.

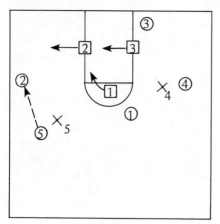

Fig. 6.18 The Three-man Triangle Zone —Two Man Man-for-man Combination Defense. Defensive Players 1, 2, and 3 Play Zone Defense While Defensive Players X4 and X5 Guard the Two Best Opponents Man-for-man. Shifting Responsibilities Are Shown on the Pass From Player X5 to X2.

One Defense or Several?

With the different positions of pick-up and various defensive maneuvers, it can be seen that quite a number of defenses are available to the basketball coach. An interesting problem faces the astute observer of the game. Is it better for a team to play one defense and spend its practice time mastering this defense so that the players will know all of the maneuvers and shifts necessary to make it successful? Or should a team play several defenses, realizing that it will not be able to perfect one particular defense as well, but expecting to gain the advantage of various strengths and weaknesses of particular opponents? Opinion varies on this question, though there are probably more coaches who adhere to the latter philosophy than the former.

The strategy of the game

7

As in all games strategy is important to both the individual player and the team. On numerous occasions, a team with inferior personnel has been able to defeat an opponent simply by the timely use of clever strategy. Since basketball has become a game of varied offenses and defenses, it is imperative that a basketball team be made up of players who have the ability to *think* in pressure situations.

Individual Strategy   The most important thing you should do strategically as an individual is to analyze your particular opponent. How good an offensive player is he and why? Can he shoot well from outside? If he cannot, then you should play him loose. Can he drive both ways? If he favors the drive to the right, then force him to drive left. This is a major weakness of most beginning players, so be alert for this strategy. How does your opponent move without the ball? If he does not move well, play him tightly and he will have a difficult time receiving the ball. He certainly cannot score if he does not get the basketball. Determine his speed. If he is fast, you will have to play him looser than normal. What about his ball handling? If he is a poor ball handler, press him tightly and force him to make mistakes.

Defensively, if he is playing you loosely, be ready to take the outside shot. Is he a "head-turner"? If he does turn to look at the ball, then be ready to cut by him for a return pass and possible score. If he plays you tightly, be ready to cut backdoor to receive a pass. When you have the ball and he plays you tightly, be prepared to drive. Watch his feet and drive to the side of his advanced foot. For example, if he has his right foot forward, drive to his right since that side will be more difficult for him to cover.

Team Strategy   Your team should use the following strategy to begin a game. You must determine what type of offense and what type of defense your opponents are playing, then use the correct offense and defense to combat each.

Are your opponents playing a zone defense or are they playing man-to-man? You can determine this by sending cutters through your opponent's defense. If they do not go with the cutters, then you know they are playing a zone defense. Are they playing a single pivot offense, a double pivot offense, or another offense? If they are playing a double pivot, make certain that your best pivot defenders are guarding their post men. Are your opponents using a fast break? If they are, make certain that you have at least two defensive players back to stop their break.

Analyze the opposing players as a team just as thoroughly as you would analyze your individual opponent. Know the weaker defensive players and attack their areas. If the team has a particularly strong rebounder, try to pull him away from the basket by letting his assigned opponent play outside. If this is a poor ball-handling team, an inexperienced, or a methodical, pattern-type team, be ready to use a full court pressing defense.

Playing for One

A fine tool is the strategy of "playing for one." This term simply means that a team plays for one last shot just prior to the end of the period. The theory is to take the shot so near the end of the period that the opponent will not have an opportunity to rebound any missed attempt and go down and score. When using this strategy most teams try to keep the ball until five to eight seconds remain in the period. A shot is then taken. This provides ample time for a chance at an offensive rebound if the shot attempt is missed. It does not, however, leave enough time for the opponent to rebound the ball and take it downcourt into scoring position. Playing for one can often mean the difference between victory and defeat in a close contest. It is a particularly useful strategy for teams who play quarters and have four different periods during the game.

When to Press

An important part of game strategy is knowing when to press or when to use any of the pressing defenses which are available. Generally pressing defenses are used when a team is trailing late in the game. Quick ball possession is a must and you cannot allow the opponent to consume time by bringing it downcourt slowly. You must challenge the ball downcourt in an effort to steal a pass or force a mistake. Sometimes a team will make the mistake of waiting too late to employ the press. Teams trailing by ten points have on occasion waited until three minutes to go to begin the press, found themselves defeated by two points, and then said "If we had just one minute more" or "If we had just started to press earlier." It is far better to begin to press too early than to wait until it is too late.

There are other reasons to press in addition to that of making an effort to come from behind. Pressing defenses are good surprise elements. They are particularly effective against the inexperienced opponent, the weak ball-handling team, the poorly conditioned team, and the team that relies heavily on set plays. If an opponent is trying to slow down the game against a fast-breaking team, the latter must have the ability to go out and harass the opposition in an effort to speed up their play.

When to Freeze

Another important part of game strategy is the use of the freeze or stall offense—controlling the ball late in the game when leading by a few points. Various offenses have been devised to enable a team to freeze the basketball. Many teams simply run their own basic formation and refuse to take any shots other than a lay-up shot.

It is rather difficult to establish an ironclad rule to determine when to begin a freeze, since the amount of lead will determine the time. If a team has a five or six point lead, its members will have a good chance of freezing the ball for two or three minutes. If the lead is only two or three points, however, three minutes is quite a long time to freeze. On the other hand, the freeze is certainly in order with a two point lead with one minute to go.

Regardless of the time a team employs the freeze, certain rules should be observed. The better ball handlers should do the majority of the ball handling. These same players should be good free-throw shooters since the defense often fouls and the freeze is of no avail if the free throw is missed. The offense should be spread, regardless of formation, and screens on the ball should be avoided to prevent any opportunities by the defense for the use of double-teaming tactics. It is wise strategy to give the ball to an offensive player who is being guarded by a slow opponent. For example, pulling the offensive center away from the basket and giving him the ball is usually a sound maneuver, since the defensive center is normally the weakest player at outside pressing defense. To employ this latter strategy, however, the offensive center must be a capable ball handler and must be a good free-throw shooter.

The freeze can be so important to a team that it is wise to make substitutions at this period in order to remove the weaker ball handlers even though they may be good scorers and rebounders. At this stage of the game possession of the ball is of paramount importance, and a mistake by a poor ball handler can prove fatal.

The Use of Time-Outs

Time-outs are very important to the success of a basketball team. Five time-outs are allowed during the regulation game and one additional time-out for each overtime period. The time-out may be used to stop a particular rally or hot streak by the opponent. Another important reason for a time-out is to change your team's offensive or defensive strategy, or to prepare for a change in the offensive or defensive strategy of the opponent. It is rather difficult to change the strategy without a time-out, for all players must be aware of the change. The time-out is also useful as a rest period, particularly late in a period.

Time-outs are of particular value during the last few minutes of play in a close game. It is during this time that various strategies and special plays are usually employed and quite a few changes are usually made. It therefore is wise to save at least two of a team's five time-outs until the last few minutes of play.

Origin and development
of basketball

8

Basketball is one of the few sports that had its start in the United States. It is truly an American game and its popularity in this country has been amazing. It was invented at Springfield College in 1891 by Dr. James Naismith, a physical education instructor who sought to develop a game for Springfield men to satisfy their desire for physical activity between the football and baseball seasons. Peach baskets were used as the first goals and a soccer ball served as the first ball. When a team scored it was necessary to bring out a ladder; some player then would climb up to remove the ball from the basket. Finally, the bottom of the peach basket was removed so that play could be speeded up. First rules were simple and the number of players allowed on each team depended on the size of the gymnasium.

Basketball was well received by participants from the beginning, and it was not long before colleges and YMCAs began forming teams. Yale fielded a team in 1892. Cornell and the University of Chicago had teams a year later.[1] Yale and Pennsylvania played the first intercollegiate basketball game in 1897.[2] After the turn of the century, the game enjoyed amazing growth. It spread rapidly from the colleges and YMCAs to the junior and senior high schools and playgrounds throughout the country, until today it is played in every village and hamlet throughout the United States and in virtually every nation.

Significant Rule Changes

A considerable amount of changes and additions to Dr. Naismith's thirteen original rules have been made over the years. Perhaps the most significant single rule change was the elimination of the center jump in the early 30s. The

1. Forrest Anderson and Stan Albeck, *Coaching Better Basketball* (New York: The Ronald Press Company, 1964), p. 5.
2. Ibid.

original game required a jump ball at center court each time a team scored. This resulted in slow play, low scoring games, and not too much spectator interest.

Two time-limitation rules have also greatly influenced the game. The first, the "ten-second rule," required the ball to be advanced into front court within ten seconds. This prevented teams from withholding the ball from play at full court distance away from their basket. The second, known as the "three-second" rule, prevented offensive players from remaining within the offensive free-throw lane for more than three seconds. This rule was passed in an effort to reduce the effectiveness of the big man.

The "bonus" free-throw rule was added in 1954. This rule gave the free-throw shooter a second shot if his first shot was successful. This led to what some critics have referred to as "a parade to the free-throw line" so the rule has now been altered—it does not go into effect until the seventh foul in each half in college basketball, and the fifth foul in high school basketball.

Another change designed to curb the effectiveness of the big man was legislated in 1957. At that time the free-throw lane was widened from six to twelve feet. Since no offensive player can remain in this lane area more than three seconds, this forced the taller player away from the basket and required him to develop more offensive maneuverability. It also helped to open up the middle area for drives. It would not be surprising to see the lane widened even more in the future.

The Jump Shot

Probably the most significant fundamental development in basketball has been the development of the jump shot which has occurred during the past twenty-five years. Prior to 1950, all one-handed shooting was done with at least one foot on the playing court. As it was discovered, however, that players could still achieve accuracy by shooting from the top of their jump thus making it far more difficult for the defense to block, more and more players began using the jump shot. As college and professional players became proficient with the jump shot high school players copied the technique and it has now become the most often used shot in the game.

Gymnasium Development

Early gymnasiums were moderate in size, had limited seating capacity, and the playing courts were smaller than the regulation floors of today. However, as rule changes increased the speed of play and the skill of the individual players improved, the popularity of the game increased; this brought on the need for larger facilities to accommodate the ever-growing number of spectators, a growth which has become increasingly apparent throughout the country. Today many colleges have gymnasiums seating from ten to fifteen thousand, and it is not uncommon for a high school gymnasium to seat four or five thousand. The University of Kentucky's new Rupp Arena seats 23,000 spectators and was

---

A recent rule change gives back an advantage tall players once had and then lost. What was this rule change and do you think it was justified?

---

sold out for the entire 1976-77 season. Though not a gymnasium, the Astrodome in Houston has been used for basketball. More than 50,000 spectators witnessed the University of Houston play UCLA there in the 1969 basketball season, while the NCAA championships there in 1971 drew more than 30,000 fans each night.

When Lew Alcindor enrolled at UCLA, rulesmakers made it illegal to "dunk" the basketball. However, the rules committee voted in the spring of 1976 to legalize the "dunk" again beginning with the 1976/77 season. With players jumping higher than ever before, this crowd-pleasing shot should play a significant part in many college teams' offenses.

The Three Most Famous Teams

The three most famous teams were the Original Celtics, the current Boston Celtics, and the Harlem Globetrotters. The Original Celtics were organized in 1914, and toured the United States for seven years, amassing an amazing record of 1,320 wins against only 66 losses. They were so strong that when they joined the American professional league they were broken up to give the other teams balance.[3]

The Boston Celtics of the National Basketball Association have dominated the game more than any other team in sports history. Coached by the "winningest coach in basketball," Arnold "Red" Auerbach, the Celtics won the 1966 NBA Championship, their eighth consecutive title and their ninth in ten years.

Without any question whatsoever, the Harlem Globetrotters, however, are the most colorful team in basketball. Organized by Abe Saperstein, the Globetrotters have combined fantastic skill with ingenious comedy to become the most well-known basketball team. They play annually before packed houses throughout the world and have done more than any other team to popularize basketball internationally.

LANGUAGE OF THE GAME

Assist—A pass that results in a score.
Backboard—The rectangular or fan-shaped board behind the goal that often is used for banking shots.
Backcourt—The half of the court that is farthest from the offensive basket.
Backdoor—A cut along the baseline when a player is being overplayed by the defense or when the defense turns to look at the ball.

---

3. John Durant and Otto Bettmann, *Pictorial History of American Sports* (New York: A. S. Barnes Co., 1952), p. 166.

Baseball Pass—A pass thrown with the same basic technique that is used when throwing a baseball. This pass is usually employed for long downcourt passes.

Basket—The goal.

Baseline—The end line running under the basket from sideline to sideline.

Blocking Off the Boards—The positioning of the defensive player in such a manner as to prevent the offensive player from going to the basket for a rebound. Also referred to as "box out" or "block out."

Bounce Pass—A pass that strikes the floor before it gets to the receiver.

Box and One—A combination defense in which four men play zone and one man plays man-for-man.

Carrying—Same as Traveling.

Center—A position usually played by the tallest player on the team.

Change of Pace—An offensive technique, usually used by the dribbler, in which speed is reduced then quickly increased to evade a defender.

Charging—Running into a player who is stationary.

Chest Pass—A two hand pass that is begun from the passer's chest and is pushed toward the receiver so that he can receive it in that same vicinity.

Clear Out—An offensive technique in which a player close to a teammate with the ball cuts away from him so that his defensive opponent cannot help out on any drive attempt.

Controlling the Boards—Gaining a majority of the rebounds.

Cut—A quick move by the offensive player, usually toward his basket.

Defensive Rebounding—Rebounding at the opponent's end of the court.

Double Dribble—Player continuing to dribble after touching the ball with both hands.

Double Pivot—A type of team offense in which two players play in the pivot area.

Double Screen—A screen set by two players.

Double Team—A defensive tactic of using two players to guard the man with the ball.

Drive—A quick dribble toward the basket in an effort to score.

Dunking—Slamming the ball down through the goal.

Fast Break—A situation in which the defensive team gains possession of the ball and moves into scoring position so quickly that its members outnumber their opponents.

Filling the Lanes—Cutting players into the three hypothetical lanes necessary for a three-on-two break situation.

Flip Pass—A pass made with one hand when exchanging the ball at close range.

Forward—A position usually played by one of the taller players which requires both shooting and rebounding ability. The forward usually plays near the sideline and toward the corner near his goal.

Free Throw—An unguarded shot from the free-throw line that is the result of a foul by the opponent.

Freezing the Ball—Withholding the ball from play without any effort to score, a tactic often used late in a game in an effort to protect a slight lead.

Fronting the Post—Guarding the pivot man in front rather than between him and the basket. It is a defensive tactic necessary to keep a good pivot man from obtaining possession of the ball close to the basket.

Give and Go—Passing the ball to a teammate and cutting hard to the basket for a return pass.

Goal Tending—Touching the ball or basket when the ball is above, on, or within either basket.

Guard—A position usually played by the smaller players. It requires good ball handling and passing as well as the ability to shoot from the outside.

High Post—An offensive player who plays near the free-throw line.

Hook Pass—A pass thrown with one hand in a sweeping motion over the head.

Hook Shot—A shot taken with one hand in a sweeping motion over the head. It is usually taken close to the basket.

Hoop—The basket, or goal.

Jump Ball—The situation involving joint possession, in which the official tosses the ball into the air and two opposing players jump in an effort to tap it toward a teammate—also referred to as a "toss up."

Jump Shot—A shot taken after the shooter has jumped into the air.

Key—The area close to the basket that includes the free-throw lane.

Lay-up Shot—A shot taken close to the basket usually with one hand.

Low Post—An offensive player who plays near the basket with his back to the basket.

Man-for-Man—A team defense in which each player is assigned a particular opponent to guard wherever this opponent may go in his offensive pattern.

Offensive Rebounding—Rebounding at the offensive end of the floor.

One-on-One—The situation in which one offensive player tries to score against one defensive player.

Outlet Pass—A pass made after a defensive rebound.

Overtime—An extra period played to break a tie score.

Palming—When the dribbler places his hand under the ball and then continues his dribble. Same as a traveling violation.

Pass—A ball thrown from one player to another.

Pass and Cut—An offensive maneuver in which the player passes to a teammate and cuts to the basket for a return pass. It is often referred to as "give and go."

Peripheral Vision—Also referred to as "split-vision"—the ability to see to the side while looking ahead.

Pick—Same as a Screen.

Pivot—Footwork that enables the ball handler to move one foot while keeping the other in the same position of contact on the floor. Also a position on the court near the basket where the tallest player is usually stationed.

Pivot Area—The area close to the basket where the center usually plays.

Pivot Man—A player who plays close to the basket.

Playing for One—The strategy of playing for one shot just prior to the end of a period.

Post—A pivot man stationed with his back to the basket and usually in a position around the foul line.

Have you mastered the game terminology? Check your definitions of these terms: flip pass, outlet pass, controlling the boards, trailer, switch.

Press Defense—A forcing type defense in which the offense is picked up farther away from the basket than normal. The press may be of half court, three-quarter court, or full court type.

Rebound—A missed shot attempt.

Reverse Dribble—The dribble technique in which the dribbler changes direction by making a complete turn so that his body will protect the ball as the dribble is continued.

Running—Same as Traveling.

Sagging Defense—A defense that drops back toward the free-throw lane area to jam the area close to the basket. It is very effective when playing against a strong pivot man.

Screen—A legal maneuver used by the offense in an effort to free a player for a shot at the basket. The screener stands in such a position that the opposing defensive player cannot get to the player in position to shoot.

Screen and Roll—An offensive technique in which the screener pivots on his inside foot and cuts to the basket. The technique is used to combat the switching defense.

Second Guard—A very popular play in basketball in which one guard passes to a forward, cuts through, and the forward hands off to the second guard coming around.

Set Shot—A shot taken from long range and a stationary position.

Single Pivot—A type of team offense in which one player plays in the pivot area.

Split-the-Post—A three-man offensive maneuver in which the ball is passed to a post man and two players scissor off him for a possible pass.

Stall—An offensive technique in which a team makes little effort to score. It is usually used by a team late in the game in an effort to kill the clock—similar to the freeze.

Stuffing—Same as Dunking.

Switch—A maneuver used by the defense to combat a screen and make possible a change of defensive assignments.

Switch Dribble—The dribble technique in which the dribbler changes dribbling hands by crossing the ball in front of his body.

Ten-second Line—The midcourt line by which the team in ball possession must advance within ten seconds.

Three-on-Two—A fast-break situation in which three offensive players attack two defensive players.

Three-second Lane—The offensive free-throw lane in which no offensive player can remain for more than three seconds at a time.

Tip-in—A quick one-handed tip of a missed field goal try that results in a score.

Trailer—An offensive player who comes downcourt after his teammates have tried to score on a three-on-two situation. The trailer can be available for an outlet pass for a quick shot or to cut through for a lay-up or a rebound.

Traveling—Taking more than one step with the ball without dribbling. Also referred to as "walking."

Turnover—Any loss of ball possession caused by a violation.

Two-on-One—A fast-break situation in which two offensive players attempt to score on one defensive player.

Violation—A rules violation that results in loss of the ball.

Weave—A type of offense involving close exchanges of the ball. The weave may be of a three-man, four-man or five-man type.

Zone Defense—A team defense in which the defensive player is assigned an area on the court to guard.

Rules of the game

9

Basketball rules in the United States are rather standardized for all levels of play. There are only a few exceptions. The major differences involve the size of the playing court and the length of playing periods; both become slightly longer as the age and skill of players increase. Rule books are published annually by the National Collegiate Athletic Bureau and by the state high school athletic associations. The following resume of the rules will suffice for normal recreational play.

PLAYING COURT, GOAL AND BALL

The recommended size of the playing court is as follows: college and professional, 50′ × 94′; high school, 50′ × 84′. Refer to figure 9.1 for full dimensions of the playing court. Notice that the free-throw lane is twelve feet in width.

The backboards to which the goals are attached are constructed of any rigid material. They shall be either of two types: (1) a rectangle 6′ × 4′, or (2) fan-shaped—54 inches wide by 35 inches high.

Each basket must be attached to the backboard parallel to the floor. The inside diameter of the basket is 18 inches, and the basket is placed 10 feet above the playing floor.

The ball must be spherical, with a maximum circumference of 30 inches and a minimum of 29½ inches and a weight of not less than twenty or more than twenty-two ounces.

PLAYERS AND SUBSTITUTES

Each team consists of five players plus substitutes. The captain of the team represents his team and may confer with an official on questions regarding interpretation or other basic information. Such discussion must be done in a courteous manner.

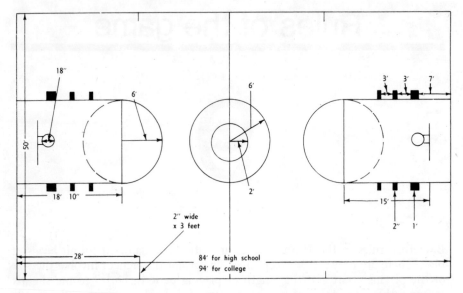

Fig. 9.1 Dimensions of a Basketball Court. All Lines Should Be 2" in Width.

When a substitute desires to enter the game, he must give his name and number to the official scorer. He may enter when he is *beckoned* by the official after the scorer has sounded the horn when the ball is dead and time is out.

Each player must wear a number on both the front and back of his shirt. The number on the back must be at least six inches high and that on the front at least four inches high. The single digit numbers 1 and 2 or any digit greater than 5 cannot be used. For example, the number 26 is illegal since one of the digits is greater than 5. The wearing of an illegal number results in the charge of a technical foul against the captain of the team.

SCORING AND TIMING

A field goal is scored when a live ball enters the basket from above and passes down through it. Such a goal from the field counts two points for the team into whose basket the ball was thrown. When a free throw is awarded for fouls, each successful free throw counts one point. If a player mistakenly shoots a field goal into his opponent's basket, the goal is counted for the opponents.

The length of the game shall be as follows:

1. College: Two halves of 20 minutes each with a 15-minute intermission between halves.
2. High school: Four quarters of 8 minutes each with a 10-minute intermission between halves and a 1-minute intermission after the first and third quarters.

3. Below high school: Four quarters of 6 minutes each with the same inter-mission as for high schools.
4. The professional game is played in four 12-minute quarters.

Each period ends when time expires, but a shot in flight counts as a score if made even after the period.

If the score is tied at the end of the regulation game one or more overtime periods are played until a winner is determined. College overtime periods are five minutes in length and high school extra periods are three minutes in length. Teams change baskets at the beginning of the first extra period but do not change again regardless of the number of extra periods which must be played.

Each team is allowed five charged time-outs during the game. For each overtime period, an additional time-out is granted each team. A technical foul is charged for each additional time-out.

A game is started by a jump ball that is taken by two opponents at the center line. After the ball is put in play, play continues and the clock runs until a violation occurs, the ball goes out of bounds, a personal foul occurs, or time-out is called.

SPECIFIC RULE DEFINITIONS

Basket is the 18-inch ring, its flanges and braces and net.

Blocking is personal contact which impedes the progress of an opponent who does not have the ball.

A *player* is in control when he is holding a live ball or dribbling it.

A *team is in control* when a player of the team has the ball and also while a live ball is being passed between teammates.

A *dribble* is ball movement by a player who taps the ball in the air or on the floor, and then touches it once or several times or catches it. Such a dribble ends when the dribbler touches the ball with both hands simultaneously, permits it to come to rest while he is in contact with it, or loses control of it.

An *air-dribble* is that part of a dribble during which the dribbler throws or taps the ball in the air and then touches it before it touches the floor.

A *foul* is an infraction of the rules, for which one or more free throws are awarded or ball possession is lost if it is a player control foul.

A *double foul* is a situation in which two opponents commit personal fouls against each other at approximately the same time.

A *multiple foul* is a situation in which teammates commit a personal foul against the same opponent at approximately the same time.

A *personal foul* results when contact is made with an opponent while the ball is alive.

A *player control foul* is a personal foul committed by a player while his team is in possession of the ball.

A *technical foul* is a foul by either a player or nonplayer which does not involve contact, or it may involve unsportsmanlike contact with an opponent while

What determines whether one or two free-throws are awarded after a personal foul? When is a bonus shot awarded?

the ball is dead; a technical foul is also awarded for other unsportsmanlike acts.

A *free throw* is awarded when a player is fouled or when a technical foul is called.

A team's *front court* is that half of the playing court nearest its own basket.

A team's *backcourt* is that half of the playing court nearest its opponent's basket.

A *held ball* or *jump ball* occurs when opponents have joint possession of the basketball, a player holds the ball in his front court while closely guarded for five seconds, or a closely guarded player dribbles for five seconds near a front court boundary.

Closely guarded is defined as within six feet.

Holding is personal contact with an opponent which prevents his freedom of movement.

A *jump ball* results when two opposing players gain joint possession of the ball. The ball is tossed by an official into the air between the two players; they jump and attempt to tap it to teammates.

A *pivot* occurs when a player in possession of the ball steps once or more in any direction while keeping one foot in contact with the floor. The foot in contact with the floor is called the pivot foot. If a player moves this pivot foot while he has the ball he is guilty of *traveling* or running with the ball.

VIOLATIONS AND PENALTIES

It is a violation to:
1. Dribble again after a player's first dribble is ended.
2. Remain for more than three seconds in the free-throw lane on the offensive end of the court while a player or his team has possession of the ball.
3. Fail to advance the ball across the midcourt line within 10 seconds.
4. Cause the ball to go backcourt after advancing it across the midcourt line.
5. Touch the basket or the ball while the ball is on or immediately above the goal.
6. Move into the circle before a jump ball is touched by one of the jumpers.
7. Step into the free-throw lane area before a free-throw attempt touches the goal or backboard.
8. Leave the designated throw in spot when throwing the ball in from out of bounds, and not throwing the ball in within five seconds.
9. Run with the ball.
10. Kick the ball or strike it with the fist.

A personal foul is called if:
1. A player holds, pushes, charges, or trips an opponent.

Can you describe two violations that could occur only within the free-throw lane?

2. A dribbler charges into an opponent or dribbles between two opponents, unless enough space is provided to enable him to do so without contact.
3. A player who screens is not stationary and does not take a position at least a normal step away from the opponent.

In general the personal foul is charged to the player who causes bodily contact, whether he is an offensive or defensive player. The penalty is one or more free throws depending upon whether the player is shooting and how many fouls his team has committed in the half. If a player is fouled in the act of shooting, two free throws are awarded unless the try is successful in which case only one free throw is awarded. If a player is fouled but not in the act of shooting he is awarded one free throw unless:

a. in high school games—the foul is his team's fifth during the half, in which case he is awarded a bonus shot if his first shot is successful.
b. in college games—if the foul is the opponent's seventh foul in the half he is awarded a bonus shot provided his first try is successful. This free-throw situation is referred to as the "one-and-one."

A player is disqualified if he commits five personal fouls in a high school or college game. Professional players are allowed six personal fouls.

A *technical foul* is awarded for situations such as delaying the game, unsportsmanlike conduct, making illegal substitutions, and using excessive time-outs. The normal penalty for a technical foul is one free throw and ball possession. However, a technical foul on a coach or on the bench results in two free throws and ball possession.

Sportsmanship in basketball

10

Though no rules are written to cover sportsmanship, it is important for the sake of both safety and enjoyment that players abide by normal rules of sportsmanship.

Players are expected to respect officials and to show courtesy to opponents at all times, and to visitors in particular. Many games are played for which one team must travel quite a distance in order to participate. These players will be unfamiliar with the community and facilities. Coaches and players of the home team should be alert to help in any way possible.

Though basketball is sometimes referred to as a noncontact sport, it is far from that; aggressive play with considerable bodily contact is the rule rather than the exception. Many opportunities are present for dirty play; such play may cause serious injury and will at least probably result in unusually rough play by both teams. Players who like to pinch the legs of opponents or jab them in the midsection when an official is not looking are a detriment to the game and should not be given the privilege of playing. Avoid dirty play at all times.

You will probably have many opportunities to play the game when no official is present. Good sportsmanship becomes doubly important at these times. Fouls must be called by the players themselves, using the honor system. Out-of-bounds and jump balls must also be called in the same manner and it is very important that you be entirely honest and fair.

Basketball is a very fast game and a player's personality can be disclosed rather quickly. You should avoid any display of temper or any emotional outbursts. The player who fails to practice self-control is looked upon with distaste by his teammates as well as by his opponents and the spectators.

Learn to be humble in victory and gracious in defeat. There is no place for the braggart in any game and the poor looser only focuses attention on his immaturity.

Remember that basketball is a team game and that team play is of utmost importance. Avoid overshooting. Look for teammates who are in a better position to shoot than you are. Applaud good plays made by your teammates and never blame your teammates for your own failures.

Facts for enthusiasts

11

National championships are conducted by several national organizations. The National Basketball Association and the American Basketball Association have world champions of their respective professional leagues. The National Collegiate Athletic Association has a national champion in three divisions. The National Association of Intercollegiate Athletics has a small college champion which is selected in a grueling 32-team, six-night tournament in Kansas City. The Amateur Athletic Union selects a national amateur champion at its tournament in Baton Rouge, Louisiana. The nation's junior colleges hold their national championships with a tournament in Hutchinson, Kansas.

High schools do not compete nationally but nearly every state holds state championship tournaments. Several states have both boys' and girls' basketball championships.

With the recent interest in athletics for women, the Association for Intercollegiate Athletics for Women now conducts a national collegiate basketball championship.

It is not uncommon for college basketball teams to play before more than 250,000 spectators in a single season. In the 1973/74 season, the University of New Mexico played before 217,928 spectators at their home games alone.[1]

Many college teams travel more than 15,000 miles in a single season. In 1973/74, the University of Hawaii and St. Mary's College each traveled more than 25,000 miles; the same season Kent State University, Adams State University, and UCLA each traveled more than 20,000 miles.[2]

Pete Maravich of Louisiana State University holds the all-time record for points scored in three years of college play. Maravich, who finished his college

1. 1974 Converse Basketball Yearbook, 53rd ed. (Malden, Mass.: Converse Rubber Co.), p. 53.
2. Ibid., pp. 52-54.

Do you know what percentage of field goal tries is considered good for a team? What is the record for successful free throws by an individual? How often does the home team win in college basketball?

---

career in 1970, scored 3,667 points in three years for an average of 44.2 points per game.[3]

Not only does Maravich hold the all-time record for points scored in three seasons, but he also holds the record for career average (44.2 points per game) and the one-season scoring record (1,381 points).[4] Frank Selvy of Furman scored 100 points against Newberry in 1954 for the single game record.[5]

In 1973/74 Arizona's Al Fleming led the nation's major colleges in field goal percentage, connecting on 136 of 204 shot attempts for a .667 percentage, while Ricky Medlock of Arkansas led the nation in free-throw percentage with 87 successful free throws in 95 attempts for a .916 percentage. Marvin Barnes of Providence grabbed 597 rebounds for an 18.7 average per game, tops nationally in that department.[6] Maryland-Eastern Shore and Texas-El Paso led Team Offense and Team Defense respectively with 97.6 and 56.5 averages per game.[7]

In 1974/75 there was only one active major college coach with more than 600 career victories—John Wooden of UCLA. Entering the season his record stood at 639-158 for a winning percentage of .802.[8] Wooden retired at the conclusion of the season after winning his tenth NCAA championship.

The home court advantage has been a major concern in basketball for many years. One survey indicated the home team came out on top 80 percent of the time in major college basketball.[9]

Several years ago coaches were well satisfied if their teams made 33 percent of their field goal tries. Today it is difficult to win unless a team shoots better than 40 percent; the nation's leading team field goal percentage leaders will shoot better than 50 percent. The individual leader shoots better than 60 percent of his field goal tries for the season, a percentage Dr. Naismith would find extremely difficult to believe. As a comparison, the Illinois basketball team in 1947/48 finished with a 15-5 record and shot .281 from the field and .565 from the free-throw line.[10] In 1973/74, Notre Dame led the nation in team field goal percentage with 1,056 field goals in 1992 attempts for a .530 percentage. Vanderbilt was the team free-throw leader with 477 free throws in 595 attempts, for a percentage of .802.[11]

3. 1975 NCAA Basketball Guide, 79th ed. (Shawnee Mission, Kan.: NCAA Publishing Service), p. 84.
4. Ibid.
5. Ibid.
6. Ibid., p. 86.
7. Ibid., p. 88.
8. 1974 Converse Yearbook, p. 14.
9. George Solomon, "There's no place like home," Basketball, p. 15.
10. "From Here and There," Athletic Journal, April 1966, p. 14.
11. 1975 NCAA Guide, p. 88.

Playing the game

12

Many opportunities are available for those who would like to play basketball, whether on the beginner, intermediate, or advanced level. One of the distinct advantages of this game over other team sports is that it can be played alone. You can purchase a rubber basketball for approximately $6.00, a goal for a similar amount, and construct a backboard with discarded lumber. A good pair of basketball shoes can be purchased for $10.00 and you are ready to play. Quite a number of shooting games are available to the individual who wants to shoot alone in his backyard. Most playgrounds throughout the country have basketball goals and most schools and colleges have gymnasiums that are open daily, thus providing many opportunities for shooting and playing the game.

For the beginner, most opportunities for playing will come on the playground with other novices. It is rather easy to find three or four other players who would like to play two-on-two or three-on-three. Enough players will often be available for five-on-five. When three-on-three is played, usually only one goal is used while five-on-five is usually played on full court.

As you improve your play, you may find that you will have the opportunity to play on your school team, either varsity or junior varsity. If you have a desire to play, most coaches will be eager to have you come out for their team, and if you are not good enough for their varsity, will be pleased to have you play junior varsity basketball. If your skill is not advanced enough for play on this level, then be sure to participate in the intramural program at your school.

If you are not in school, you will find many opportunities for play in playground leagues, church leagues, or YMCA leagues. Check with your local recreation department or your local YMCA for full information as to what leagues are available.

Basketball is played the year round, and facilities for the game are improving constantly. If you have a sincere desire to play the game, you will have no trouble finding opportunities. Work at the game daily and play as often as possible and you will be pleasantly surprised at the results you will accomplish.

Appendix: Questions and answers

MULTIPLE CHOICE

1. A distinct advantage of the Shuffle Offense is:
   a. the middle is kept clear to allow quick cuts to the basket
   B. players do not have to return to their original positions to continue the offense
   c. quick cuts and stationary screens enable the offense to get free for numerous set shots
   d. good ball-handling combined with quick cuts to the basket result in numerous lay-up shots   (pp. 40-41)

2. The box and one is used when:
   a. the opposing team is a pattern-type team
   b. the opposing team has one player who is a good shooter
   C. the opposing team has an unusually high-scoring individual
   d. the opposing team has an inexperienced player who can be left unguarded
                                                                                    (pp. 58-59)

3. The chief advantage of the hook shot is:
   a. it can be taken quickly   C. it is difficult to defend
   b. it can be easily learned   d. it is very accurate   (p. 22)

4. The baseball pass is used:
   A. to pass to teammates cutting downcourt
   b. when freezing the ball
   c. in close exchanges of the ball
   d. when feeding the cutter off a "split the post" maneuver   (p. 23)

5. A chief disadvantage of the hook pass is:
   a. it cannot be used to pass over a defensive player
   B. it is difficult to control
   c. it is difficult to receive
   d. it usually is thrown too hard   (p. 24)

6. The most common offense known to basketball is:
   A. single pivot offense   c. weave
   b. double pivot offense   d. tandem pivot offense   (p. 37)

7. The double pivot offense is used when:
   a. a team has good ball-handlers and desires to control the ball
   b. a team has excellent shooting guards and desires to set up screens for outside shots

C. a team has two tall players they would like to keep close to the basket

d. a team has excellent speed and desires to keep the middle open for quick cuts to the basket   (p. 38)

8. A field goal scores:
   A. two points   b. one point   c. three points   (p. 1)

ANSWER THE FOLLOWING

9. Explain the difference between the speed dribble and the control dribble. (The speed dribble is used when you must advance the ball quickly downcourt and no defensive players are harassing you. The control dribble is used when defensive players are near and the ball must be protected.)   (p. 24)

10. What is the primary purpose of the pivot? (To enable the ball-handler to pivot his body between his opponent and the basketball to better protect the ball.)   (p. 16)

11. Which method of free-throw shooting is most popular today? Why? (Most players now use the push-shot method. This is because the same basic shot which is used in regular play can also be used from the free-throw line and the additional practice that would be required to develop the underhand method is, as a result, not necessary.)   (pp. 9-10)

12. What will be the result if the bounce pass strikes the floor too far away from the receiver? (The ball will float into the air and be easily intercepted.)   (pp. 13-14)

13. What is the key to a successful fast break? (The speed with which the outlet pass is made after a rebound.)   (p. 45)

14. Name three types of teams the pressing defense is useful against:
    a. weak ball-handling team   c. poorly conditioned team
    b. inexperienced team   d. methodical pattern type team   (pp. 52-53)

TRUE OR FALSE

t F   15. The basket or goal is a cylinder approximately 20″ in diameter.   (p. 1)

t F   16. A free-throw from a technical foul scores two points.   (p. 1)

T f   17. A free-throw from a personal foul scores one point.   (p. 1)

T f   18. The ball can be advanced quicker by passing than by dribbling.   (p. 1)

t F   19. A team is composed of six players—three guards, two forwards, and a center.
                                                                                 (p. 1)

t F   20. In a man-for-man defense, each player has the responsibility of guarding any man in his area of the court.   (p. 2)

t F   21. A forward needs to excel in ball-handling and dribbling more than in rebounding.   (p. 3)

t F   22. The palms of the hand should touch the basketball only when shooting.
                                                                                 (p. 3)

t F   23. The lay-up shot should be broad-jumped rather than high-jumped.   (p. 5)

T f   24. The jump shot did not become popular until the 1950s.   (p. 6)

t F   25. A good jump shooter will practice shooting the jump shot while falling backwards and sideways.   (p. 7)

t F   26. When you receive a pass, dribble immediately to prevent defensive pressure.
                                                                                 (p. 43)

T f   27. A pivot made on the heel rather than the ball of the foot is a violation.   (p. 16)

t F   28. After rebounding a missed shot, it is a foul to move the elbows back and forth even though no contact is made.   (p. 17)

t F   29. Proper defensive stance requires the back to be bent.   (p. 18)

T f   30. Defensive footwork is similar to that employed by the boxer.   (p. 19)

T f   31. Generally, proper defensive position requires the defensive player to remain between his opponent and the basket at all times.   (p. 19)

T f   32. It is very important to protect the baseline in team defensive play.   (p. 50)

T f   33. A good man-for-man defense will prevent the pass into the pivot area.   (p. 50)

T f   34. In a zone defense, each player is assigned a particular area of the floor to defend.   (p. 2)

t F   35. The hook shot is taken from close range and is begun while facing the basket.   (p. 22)

t F   36. Few hook shooters use the backboard.   (p. 22)

t F   37. When throwing the baseball pass, keep the weight on the back foot until after the ball leaves the hand.   (p. 23)

T f   38. The switch dribble can be made quicker than the reverse dribble.   (p. 26)

T f   39. Throughout the reverse dribble the body is kept between the ball and the defensive player.   (p. 26)

t F   40. Adolph Rupp popularized the Shuffle Offense in the South.   (p. 40)

T f   41. The Shuffle Offense requires all players to play all positions.   (p. 40)

t F   42. The first option of the Shuffle Offense is a pass to the forward cutting into the pivot area.   (p. 41)

T f   43. The third option of the Shuffle Offense is a pass to the center at the top of the circle.   (p. 41)

T f   44. The weave has been popular primarily in the eastern sector of the United States.   (p. 41)

t F   45. Players dislike the fast break because of the ball-handling and conditioning required.   (p. 45)

t F   46. If your defensive opponent has his right foot forward, drive to his left since that side will be more difficult for him to cover.   (p. 60)

t F   47. The strategy of "playing for one" should be used early in the game to take advantage of the opponent's weak defensive players.   (p. 61)

t F   48. Good screens are very important when freezing the ball.   (p. 62)

t F   49. A team should attempt to save one time-out for the last few minutes of play when strategy is so important.   (p. 63)

T f   50. Yale was the first college to field a basketball team.   (p. 64)

T f   51. The "bonus" free-throw rule goes into effect after the sixth foul in college basketball and after the fourth foul in high school basketball.   (p. 65)

t F   52. College teams play two halves of sixteen minutes each with a fifteen minute half-time intermission.   (p. 72)

t F   53. A multiple foul is a situation in which two opponents commit personal fouls against each other at approximately the same time.   (p. 73)

T f   54. It is a violation to touch the basket while the ball is immediately above the goal.   (p. 74)

t F   55. It is not a violation to strike the ball with the fist.   (p. 74)

T f   56. The reverse dribble affords better ball protection than the switch dribble.   (p. 26)

t F   57. When freezing the ball, the center should never handle the ball.   (p. 62)

t F   58. Basketball was invented as a substitute for the rougher game of football.   (p. 64)

t F   59. The "ten-second" rule requires that the ball be passed from one player to another within ten seconds.   (p. 65)

T f   60. The jump shot is considered the most effective shot in basketball.   (p. 6)

T f   61. The popularity of the underhand free-throw has declined in recent years.
(pp. 9-10)

T f   62. The actual floor position of the individual defensive player will vary with the position of the ball. (p. 19)

T f   63. Your target for a lay-up shot should be a spot on the backboard 12 to 15 inches above the goal. (p. 4)

COMPLETION

64. The three basic shots are: (lay-up, jump and free-throw). (p. 4)

65. When using the backboard for a lay-up shot, the target should be a spot on the backboard approximately (12-15″) above the goal. (p. 4)

66. Name some common errors made in shooting the lay-up shot. (pp. 5-6)

67. The jump shot should be practiced from three situations:
    a. (from a stationary position)
    b. (after a dribble)
    c. (after cutting to receive a pass). (p. 7)

68. The two major styles of free-throw shooting are: (underhand and one-hand push).
(p. 9)

69. The most accurate method of free-throw shooting has proven to be the (underhand) method. (p. 9)

70. Bunny Leavitt set the world free-throw record when he scored (499) consecutive free-throws. (p. 9)

71. What is the secret to good shooting? (Practice) (p. 4)

72. What is the major cause of fumbled passes? (Not watching the ball all the way into the hands) (p. 12)

73. The three types of passes essential for all players are: (chest, bounce and flip). (p. 13)

74. The (bounce) pass is a good pass to use in order to pass by a taller opponent or to feed a teammate who is in close to the basket. (p. 13)

75. The (flip) pass is necessary during a close exchange of the ball. (p. 13)

76. Proper pivoting techniques must be mastered in order to avoid (traveling or walking) violations. (p. 16)

77. Keeping the body between an opponent and the basket on a rebound attempt is referred to as (blocking or screening) off the boards. (p. 17)

78. Individual defensive ability depends on four major factors: (stance, footwork, position and vision). (p. 18)

79. Proper defensive footwork centers around the (slide) step. (p. 18)

80. The range of the hook shot is no more than (12) feet from the basket. (p. 22)

81. Adolph Rupp maintains that if there is a secret in successful basketball that secret is drilling on (fundamentals). (p. 31)

82. The tandem post offense requires a team to have an outstanding (guard). (p. 40)

83. Coach (Dean Smith) has probably done more to stimulate interest in the passing game offense than any other coach. (p. 42)

84. Defense can be the great (equalizer). (p. 48)

85. When a man-for-man defense picks up the opponent at midcourt it is referred to as a (half-court man-for-man press) defense. (p. 51)

86. Foremost attention of the zone defense is on the (ball). (p. 52)

87. The man-for-man defense and zone defense have been combined to result in a (combination) defense. (p. 58)

88. When the opposing team has two unusually high scoring individuals, a (triangle and two) defense may be effective. (p. 59)

89. (Five) time-outs are allowed during a regulation game. (p. 73)

90. (One) additional time-out is allowed for each extra period. (p. 73)

91. Basketball was invented in (1891) at (Springfield) College. (p. 64)

92. The inventor of basketball was (Dr. James Naismith). (p. 64)

93. The first collegiate game was played in 1897 between (Yale) and (Pennsylvania). (p. 64)

94. The most significant single rule change over the years was the elimination of the (center jump). (p. 64)

95. The "three-second" rule was passed in an effort to reduce the effectiveness of the (big man). (p. 65)

96. The free-throw lane is (twelve) feet in width. (pp. 65, 71)

97. The most significant fundamental development in basketball has been the development of the (jump shot). (p. 65)

98. The three most famous basketball teams were: (Original Celtics, Boston Celtics and the Harlem Globetrotters). (p. 66)

99. The basket is (ten) feet above the playing floor. (p. 71)

100. The diameter of the basket is (18) inches. (p. 71)

101. (Pete Maravich) holds the major college individual scoring record for a college career. (p. 77)

102. During the 1964-65 season, the home team came out on top (80) percent of the time in major college basketball. (p. 78)

103. Today it is difficult to win unless a team shoots better than (40) percent. (p. 78)

104. The shot taken with the shooting arm fully extended is called the (hook) shot. (p. 22)

105. The rules of the game allow the player holding the ball to step in any direction with one foot while keeping the other foot, called the (pivot) foot, at its point of contact with the floor. (p. 16)

ANSWERS TO EVALUATION QUESTIONS

*No Answer

Page		Answer and Page Reference
7	*	
8	*	
9	*	

10 The underhand method has been found to be more accurate. Most players prefer the push-shot method because it is the same basic shot used in regular play and it eliminates the additional practice required to develop the underhand method of free-throw shooting. (pp. 9-10)

14 *

15 *

16 *

19 The player should watch his opponent's stomach or midsection. (p. 20)

23 *

28 *

30 *

32 The higher trajectory (A) is better when closely guarded. It is also more accurate but requires greater strength.

41 The shuffle offense is well suited to a team with balanced height. The shuffle offense requires more player versatility since all players must learn all positions. (pp. 40-41)

45 B should pass the ball to the middle to player A.

46 The four situations that determine when to fast break are: (1) a missed field goal or free throw by the opponents; (2) a successful field goal or free throw by the opponents; (3) a bad pass, double dribble, or other loss of ball possession by the opponents; and (4) a jump-ball situation. The key to success in fast breaking is the speed with which the outlet pass is made after a rebound. (p. 45)

50 B should pass the ball to A or C and cut. A should clear to the opposite side of the floor taking his man out of the play.

57 *

58 The box and one is used when the opposing team's high scorer is a forward or center. The diamond and one is used when the opposing team's high scorer is a guard. (p. 59)

66 A recent basketball rule change again made the "dunk" legal.* (p. 66)

69 *

74 Whether one or two free throws are awarded is determined by how many fouls have been committed previously in the half by the team making the foul, whether the player fouled was in the act of shooting, and, if so, whether the goal was made. A bonus shot is awarded the player fouled while not in the act of shooting provided he makes his free throw and if, in high school games, it is the offending team's fifth foul during the half or, in college games, it is the opponent's seventh foul. (p. 75)

75 A player may not remain in the lane for more than three seconds when his team has possession of the ball. A player may not step into the lane before a free-throw attempt touches the goal or backboard. (p. 74)

78 A good percentage of field goal tries is considered to be better than 40 percent. Bunny Leavitt holds the record for successful free throws with 499 consecutive free throws. It has been estimated that the home team wins 80 percent of the time. (pp. 9, 78)

Index